P9-DWX-973

TWAYNE'S WORLD AUTHORS SERIES

A Survey of the World's Literature

Sylvia E. Bowman, Indiana University

GENERAL EDITOR

CANADA

Joseph Jones, University of Texas

EDITOR

Frederick Philip Grove

(TWAS 246)

TWAYNE'S WORLD AUTHORS SERIES (TWAS)

*The purpose of TWAS is to survey the major writers—
novelists, dramatists, historians, poets, philosophers,
and critics—of the nations of the world. Among the
national literatures covered are those of Australia,
Canada, China, Eastern Europe, France, Germany,
Greece, India, Italy, Japan, Latin America, the
Netherlands, New Zealand, Poland, Russia, Scandi-
navia, Spain, and the African nations, as well as
Hebrew, Yiddish, and Latin Classical literatures. This
survey is complemented by Twayne's United States
Authors Series and English Authors Series.*

*The intent of each volume in these series is to present
a critical-analytical study of the works of the writer;
to include biographical and historical material that
may be necessary for understanding, appreciation,
and critical appraisal of the writer; and to present
all material in clear, concise English—but not to
vitiate the scholarly content of the work by doing so.*

Frederick Philip Grove

By MARGARET R. STOBIE

University of Manitoba

Twayne Publishers, Inc.   ::   New York

Copyright © *1973 by Twayne Publishers, Inc.*
All Rights Reserved

Library of Congress Catalog Card Number: 72-075114

PR
6013
·R84
Z79

MANUFACTURED IN THE UNITED STATES OF AMERICA

66771

To Bill

Acknowledgments

I acknowledge my gratitude to the many people in many places in Manitoba and Ontario who received me so graciously and talked so well of their memories of Grove, and to the others from Kelowna, British Columbia, to Teheran, who obligingly answered my letters.

I acknowledge permission from the Grove estate for all of the quotations from the writing of Frederick Philip Grove that appear in this book. I acknowledge permission also from McClelland & Stewart for quotations from all books under their imprint and further, for quotations from their correspondence with Grove. The Macmillan Company of Canada gave me permission to use the quotations from their correspondence that appear herein, and Queen's University gave me permission to quote from papers in their Lorne Pierce Collection. I was given special permission by Mrs. Therese E. Thomson, Director of the Canadian Writers' Foundation, Inc., to examine and quote from their records of Grove as a beneficiary of the foundation.

It also gives me pleasure to acknowledge the kindness of a number of librarians, some of whom went far beyond the call of their profession in helping me: Mr. David Wilder, former Director of Libraries at the University of Manitoba, and his assistants, Mr. John Muchin, Special Collections, and Miss Pamela Moore, Interlibrary Loans; Miss Rose Mary Gibson, Assistant Archivist, Queen's University; Mr. Erik Spicer, Librarian of Parliament; Miss C. J. Pert, Winnipeg Public Library; and various good people in the National Archives of Canada, and in the Provincial Library and the Public Archives of Manitoba.

I appreciated the friendly cooperation that I received from a number of official bodies: in Ottawa, from the Department of Manpower and Immigration and from the Department of the Secretary of State; in Manitoba from the Department of Youth and Education and from officials of the several school districts in which Grove taught. Within the University of Manitoba, I wish to say a special thanks to Mr. Garth McLeod, who guided me through the mazes of the Comptroller's Office, and to Professor Doris Saunders who contributed her special knowledge to the Foreword.

Finally, I acknowledge most happily the generosity of the University of Manitoba in giving me a sabbatical year in which to do this study, and that of the Canada Council in giving me a research grant to support it.

Foreword

The Grove Collection

When the University of Manitoba sought to acquire the Papers left by the Canadian novelist, Frederick Philip Grove, it did so to honor two people: the first, its late librarian, Elizabeth Dafoe, and the second, a distinguished writer, Grove himself, to whom it had already given an honorary degree. The project was first discussed at a meeting of the Elizabeth Dafoe Memorial Committee on May 19, 1961. It was agreed that as chairman, I should write to Mrs. Grove who was then living in Simcoe, Ontario, about the possibility of our obtaining the manuscripts or typescripts of Grove's published and unpublished novels, short stories, articles, journals, notebooks, and letters. Mrs. Grove's initial reaction was expressed in her reply on May 29, 1961:

> While reading your letter, first a big lump rose in my throat and then tears ran down my cheeks. I am very deeply touched and very grateful to you and the Elizabeth Dafoe Memorial Committee for wishing to honour my husband in this beautiful and enduring way. I shall be happy to cooperate in every way.
>
> I have a considerable amount of material—including hand-written manuscripts of both published and unpublished books. I do not know the selling price of manuscripts, etc., but that, no doubt, could be found out. I should certainly have great satisfaction to see this, "The Grove Collection," completed during my lifetime.

On June 7, I asked Mrs. Grove if she would make a catalogue of her husband's papers, and on June 14. 1961, she complied by sending a list of the unpublished literary work of Frederick Philip Grove, as it had been left to her in his will:

I. Unpublished finished books:
  1. The Weatherhead Fortunes
  2. The Poet's Dream (or The Canyon)
  3. Jane Atkinson
  4. Murder in the Quarry
  5. Tales from the Margin
  6. A Volume of Poetry
II. Unfinished novels *in handwriting:*
  1. The House of Stene
  2. The Lean Kine
  3. Heart's Desire (or Two Lives)
  4. Wilfrid and Barbara
  5. The Hillside
  6. The Seasons (typed—last novel)
III. Forty-one short stories (not contained in Tales from the Margin) La Grande Passion (a long short story)

As for letters, she said, "I have those written to my husband by publishers and friends since the appearance of *Over Prairie Trails,* but of *his* letters I have only those written to me during his three Canadian Club lecture tours, as well as those written to me before our marriage." In the same letter of June 14, 1961, she asked if it was the wish of our committee to make "this Grove Collection the only one in Canada," to which I naturally replied, "Yes, indeed."

In order to establish a fair price for the purchase of the Papers, on July 17, our president, Dr. Hugh Saunderson, asked Dr. W. S. Wallace, ex-librarian of the University of Toronto, if he would act for both parties. Dr. Saunderson made it clear that the collection was to include not only the literary works of a formal nature but other material such as: "letters, notes or memoranda . . . as the value of the Collection to scholars would be less if the informal papers were missing." Mrs. Grove accepted the president's choice of an intermediary with the proviso that she be at liberty to refuse what she might consider "an inadequate offer." This was understandable as she was nearing the age of seventy and still teaching.

On an invitation from Mrs. Grove I went to Simcoe on August 29, 1961, and was most graciously received by a very sprightly person. While her white farmhouse had not become a literary shrine, others, too, had been shown the large and airy study with the broad double-sized desk upon which Grove had written his later works. There, too, were kept some of the "scribblers" in which Grove wrote in an extremely small hand, sometimes in pencil, and sometimes in ink, the first versions of his novels. Occasionally, when he came to the end of an exercise book, probably to conserve paper, he turned the book and wrote across the previous pages. Mrs. Grove explained that she kept the more important manuscripts in a bank vault and that she would be relieved to find a safe depository for her husband's papers. Fire and theft were the obvious hazards. She said that she had a dossier of the letters that had passed between Professor Arthur Phelps and her husband, and between Professor Watson Kirkconnell and her husband when these men were teaching at Wesley College, now the University of Winnipeg. She also had letters from the firm of McClelland & Stewart regarding their publication of *Over Prairie Trails*. She indicated that she would most likely leave in her will to our university the letters she had received from her husband as she would like our collection to be definitive. She assumed that the royalties from her husband's books would remain with her, and on her death would go to her son, Leonard. There was no doubt during my visit to Mrs. Grove that the University of Manitoba's recognition of her husband's work brought her real joy.

In September 1961, Dr. Wallace assessed the Grove Collection at $12,000, probably thinking that our university wished to acquire the full rights to the unpublished material from which it would later receive royalties. The vice-president of our university suggested that the sum of $9,000 would, under the circumstances, be a fairer price. In view of the fact that the keepers of the Elizabeth Dafoe Fund had in their possession only $2,000, black melancholy settled on the committee. President Saunderson, however, began to seek funds from various business and philanthropic organizations, even though his difficulty was compounded by the fact that most of these had been solicited for the university's Capital Grants Program on the understanding that the same donors be not approached again. What was worse, neither the Winnipeg Foundation nor the Canada Council considered that our project came under their terms of reference. About six months later Mrs. Grove wrote to commiserate with us in our seemingly fruitless attempts to raise money, and intimated that she wished she were in a position to make us a gift of the collection. At last in May 1962, thanks to grants from the president's Contingency Fund, and from the University Library, we were able to offer her the sum of $10,000 with the hope that she would find it "adequate." She did, as shown in her letter of June 4, 1962: "I, too, am very happy that the University is now able to conclude the negotiations regarding my husband's MSS. The price of $10,000 is acceptable, and I shall be so relieved to know that they are in the keeping of the University of Manitoba." A legal agreement was executed on June 21, 1962, and on July 17 a check for the full amount was sent to the Crown Trust Company of Brantford, Ontario, to be credited to the account of Catherine Grove.

In November the University Library proudly arranged a display of some of the Grove Papers, and the *Winnipeg Free Press* published a couple of articles describing it. These I sent to Mrs. Grove and on November 21, 1962, received from her an enthusiastic reply, "It was so nice to hear from you and all the news re the Grove MSS. It is all extremely interesting, and I should very much like to see the display." Thoughtfully she sent to the University two photographs of her husband: one informal, showing Grove in a turtleneck sweater, and with his crutch in the background; the other formal, and better known, of Grove wearing a high, stiff, white collar. When we learned that Mrs. Grove intended going to Saskatchewan to visit an elder sister whom she had not seen for forty years, we invited her to stay in Winnipeg to see the Grove display. She accepted, and on her return to Simcoe she wrote on January 12, 1963, "You gave me such a wonderful time in Winnipeg that I find it difficult to get down to earth."

To thank me for a copy of my paper given to the annual meeting of the Bibliographical Society of Canada on July 15, 1963, she wrote one of her most uninhibited letters:

I was most tremendously interested! How great an interest therefore to those who have not seen or heard too much of this acquisition by the University if they are interested in Grove. I laughed when as I read serious discussion, then suddenly, "the strapping of a tent onto the bumper of a car." I had often thought that if ever these MSS. were going to be read for study, there would be many puzzling surprises. I also see that my pencil remarks here and there, instead of being helpful, as at the time I hoped they would be, are confusing. . . . I am truly grateful that all this new interest has happened in my life-time. And as you say, on several occasions,—maybe I'll still see something published!

I am alone, of course, at present. So here I sit, now certainly an old lady (though frankly I do not feel old), knitting (as old ladies should) and reliving those years when I was young and so busy, and so ambitious for Phil's success. I'm satisfied and grateful. It is a wonderful feeling! And in large part due to the University of Manitoba, and for such things as you have done in preparing this paper.

Thanks to Mrs. Grove's intercession Professor Carleton Stanley, one of Grove's friends, promised to deposit his correspondence with, or about, Grove in our collection. Professor Stanley told her that he still had about thirty letters "from Phil, or from you writing for Phil," together with two others, one from Henry Burton, and one from Hugh S. Eayrs of Macmillans—"very germane to the record." These letters are now among the Grove Papers.

Suddenly, on April 27, 1964, I received an exciting telegram from Mrs. Grove: "CONTACT MY BROTHER A BIG FIND OF MSS. LETTER FOLLOWING." Feeling like a Yale University sleuth on the trail of the Boswell Papers, I telephoned Mrs. Grove's brother, Mr. John Wiens, and was invited to come at once to his home in south Winnipeg. He said he had found in an old trunk manuscripts that Grove had given him for safekeeping and that he had forgotten about. Mrs. Grove's letter of April 27, 1964, is self-explanatory:

This is exciting news! That must be the original MS. of *Settlers*, as well as—No—the *Pioneers* Jack speaks of I believe is part of *Settlers*. I shall anxiously wait to hear from you. And 16 hand written scribblers! Now if you have picked them up please tell me as much as you can by letter. In fact, do not give them to the U. until I approve. That is fair, isn't it? Also, tell me, by our contract they don't really belong to the U.? Do they? I wept. It is as if I had sudden contact with Phil.

I had taken the carton containing the scribblers to the University Library, but had made it clear that they belonged to Mrs. Grove. As the existence of these manuscripts had not been known when the original contract was drawn up, the university agreed that they did indeed belong to Mrs. Grove and that it should purchase them from her. On May 12, 1964, she expressed her willingness to sell them:

Yes, of course, I shall give Manitoba U. the first option. Your suggestion of a new agreement which will include whatever papers turn up in the future is good. I approve. Something could turn up when I'm gone. And, I, too, would like to have all material in one place. As for money, be as generous as you can afford to. I need a new roof on my house which has been some concern, and then something like this happens—and I feel I have so much to be thankful for.

She accepted the university's offer of $1,000, and that summer she came to see the new Grove Papers housed by now in the Rare Book Room of the Elizabeth Dafoe Library. On this last visit she went on to Rapid City, Manitoba, and of her day there she wrote, "It all looked so bleak and lonely. And yet the people were all so wonderfully, honestly happy to see me. It was quite an experience."

Mrs. Grove continued to live in the white farmhouse on the outskirts of Simcoe until her death in January, 1972. Her son, Mr. A. Leonard Grove, kindly gave me permission to quote from his mother's letters for this note on the Grove Collection.

Doris B. Saunders
Professor Emeritus

University of Manitoba
Winnipeg, May 1972

Preface

The man who came to call himself Frederick Philip Grove delighted to surround himself with romantic mystery and to raise teasing queries as to where he came from, what he had been, or what name he was born with. (On one occasion he said it was Gropfe.) Now, however, the mystery is being dissipated by the fine work of Douglas O. Spettigue who is engaged in writing the account of "F.P.G.—The European Years." In the *Queen's Quarterly* for April 1972, Spettigue announced his findings about F.P.G.'s identity: that his name was Felix Paul Greve, that he was German, that his father "was a minor official in the collections department of the city transport system" in Hamburg, that he married in Germany, and that he emigrated to North America "probably late in 1909 or early 1910." [1] So far, the earliest part of Grove's life on this continent that can be substantiated is his arrival in the village of Haskett, Manitoba, in the New Year of 1913 to begin a new and pseudonymous life. And it is that life— his life as a writer in Canada—that this book is concerned with.

The very lack of a reliable account of Grove's early life, however, made it the more important to examine all available records that do exist in order to gain some background for the understanding of the writer and his work. To that end, I gathered as much firsthand information as I could search out both from Grove's acquaintances, colleagues, and pupils who are still living, and from contemporary written records in local newspapers, in periodicals, in a very considerable body of Grove's correspondence with friends and publishers, in school records, and in various files that are preserved in the National Archives.

The immediacy of this body of material gives a lively picture of the writer-in-progress from the obscure small-town schoolteacher who published *Over Prairie Trails* in 1922, through his astonishing rise within six years to be a national figure, a "famous author" bowing to standing ovations from coast to coast. And when the frenzy of adulation had passed, he was the recipient of every honor that the Canadian world of letters could bestow. Grove's rise was partly the result of the zealous support of A. L. Phelps and other friends, and partly a phenomenon of the strong Canadianism movement of the 1920's that saw in Grove one who might fulfill the dream of a noble Canadian literature. To his audiences he was, in addition, the embodiment of The Immigrant, both their prick of conscience and their pride in the New Canadian. Such was the profile of this writer in his time. As a background for that profile, I have used Phelps's letters during his efforts to get Grove established, which Mrs. Phelps generously gave me permission to quote from, and I have given a brief account of the Canadianism movement and Grove's connection with it, which he sometimes noted very candidly in his letters to his wife during the Canadian Club tours, letters of which Mr. Leonard Grove kindly gave copies to the Grove Collection.

Grove's habit of placing his themes against various settings as he became familiar with them, and of picking up details of lives and of physical surroundings as either examples or embellishments seemed to me to make it important to give some account of local circumstances, which I have done with the Mennonite Reserve, the people of the Marsh, the events in Rapid City, and Grove's life in Simcoe. This material provides not only a background for his fictional shaping of fact in the novels but also a foreground for assessing the account of the people and places that he gave in the latter part of *In Search of Myself.*

Relations with publishers are always an important aspect of a writer's career, but they assume particular importance with Grove both because he ran almost the whole gamut of Canadian publishing houses and because he himself became a publisher for a brief time. As a result of Mrs. Grove's kindness in allowing two sealed boxes of correspondence within the Grove Collection to be opened last year, I gained a view of Grove and the publishing world that had some unexpected turns in it.

I have given the main emphasis and the greatest space to the decade 1919–29, in which eight of Grove's published books were written, two others begun, and further manuscripts completed which, though they were never published, were submitted for publication at various times. It also includes the writing of most of the short stories and the verse. I think it is reasonably clear, from remarks that Mrs. Grove has made both in conversation and in the CBC Symposium, "In Search of Frederick Philip Grove," that Grove did not start his Canadian writing career until 1919. In the Symposium she said, for instance, that he had begun on *A Search for America* before *Over Prairie Trails* was published, or in other words *Trails* was in the publisher's hands when he began *A Search*. This is the kind of thing that I think a wife would know; they had then been married for five years. From references in letters to Grove from Phelps and from publishers, I have suggested a rough chronological order for Grove's writing during these years which seems to me to reveal, in rather interesting fashion, some of the large designs that he had sketched for his writing, designs that appear again in the works of the later years.

Other contemporary records give a significant perspective on these designs and on Grove's intellectual background. A little group of his letters from Winkler that I discovered in the summer of 1970, two articles that he published in 1914, and information from his pupils of that day all reveal very clearly the professional teacher trained in the concepts of nineteenth-century German educational philosophy. That philosophy stemmed from Rousseau, it held the unity of nature as a doctrine, it emphasized the combination of mathematics and nature study as the fundamental one for education, it believed firsthand observation of nature to be not only educationally but morally superior to learning from books, through Froebel it expanded into symbolism, with Herbart it saw the child as passing through the "cultural epochs" of human history, and it conceived of "natural" education as the regenerative means whereby society could be led back to its intended greatness. It was both pedagogical theory and religious conviction. It was the relevant core of Grove's training and thinking, and, to a large degree, this educational philosophy determined the themes of his writing.

The whole body of contemporary material contributes to an understanding of Grove's work, both his successes and his failures. Grove commands attention as a literary phenomenon of the 1920's; he commands attention because, by his persistence and the devotion of publishers, he managed to get twelve books published in his lifetime. He deserves attention because of a couple of those books and a number of isolated passages.

MARGARET STOBIE

University of Manitoba
May, 1972

Contents

Chronology

1879   Felix Paul Greve born February 14 to Charles Edward and Bertha Greve, at Radomno, on the Polish-Prussian border, while they were on a journey from their home in Schwerin.

1881   The Greves moved to Hamburg where Herr Greve was a minor official in the city transport system, and where Felix got his schooling.

1898   Entered Bonn University. Frau Greve died.

1902   Married. Began as free-lance writer and translator.

1909/1912?   Emigrated to North America.

1913   January–June, taught school at Haskett, Manitoba. June, passed the first half of Grade XII Teachers' Course. Summer, attended bilingual Normal School at Morden. September, appointed principal of Winkler school.

1914   August 2, married Tena Wiens. November, published "The Entrance Examinations," and "Jean Jacques Rousseau als Erzieher."

1915   July, moved to Virden, Manitoba, as high school mathematics teacher. August 5, daughter, Phyllis May, born. September, began university course as extramural student. April, passed second-year university examinations.

1916   August, moved to Gladstone as principal of the high school. April, awarded $150 scholarship in third-year French.

1917   July–August, taught at Leifur school. Mrs. Grove at Falmouth school. December, resigned from Gladstone school.

1918   March, began teaching at Ferguson school, living at Falmouth.

1919   August, moved to Eden as principal of the consolidated school. November 1, resigned from Eden school.

1920   January, moved to Ashfield where Mrs. Grove taught. Injury to Grove's back, prolonged disability.

1921   August, returned to Eden as principal; Mrs. Grove also teaching there. December, received certificate of naturalization.

1922   May, received bachelor of arts degree from University of Manitoba. June 1, released from Eden school. Summer, moved to Rapid City as principal of the high school; Mrs. Grove teaching in the public school. October, *Over Prairie Trails* published.

1923   November, *The Turn of the Year* published. December, resigned from Rapid City school.

1924   January, returned to teaching until June.

1925   October, *Settlers of the Marsh* published.

1927   July 20, death of May. October, *A Search For America* published.

1928   Spring, Canadian Club tour in Ontario. Fall, Canadian Club tour in the western provinces. October, *Our Daily Bread* published.

1929   January–June, associate editor, *The Canadian Nation.* Spring, tour of eastern Canada. March, *It Needs to Be Said* published. September, left Rapid City. December, moved into Ottawa to join Graphic Publishers.

1930   October, *The Yoke of Life* published. October 14, son, Arthur Leonard, born.

1931   Left Graphic Publishers. October, moved from Ottawa to Simcoe.

1933   January, *Fruits of the Earth* published.

1934   Awarded the Lorne Pierce Gold Medal by the Royal Society of Canada.

1939   *Two Generations* published: January, author's limited edition; July, trade edition. Given an honorary life membership in the Canadian Authors' Association.

1941   Elected a Fellow of the Royal Society of Canada.

1942   August, defeated as a Co-operative Commonwealth Federation (CCF) candidate in the provincial election.

1944   March, made a beneficiary of the Canadian Writers' Foundation, Inc. April, suffered a stroke. December, *The Master of the Mill* published.

1946   May, honorary degree from the University of Manitoba. October, *In Search of Myself* published.

1947   January, *Consider Her Ways* published. July, received the governor-general's award for *In Search of Myself,* nonfiction.

1948   Died, August 19.

PART I

The Outlander

CHAPTER 1

The Mennonite Reserve

O N January 3, 1913, another new teacher stood in front of the twenty children, grades 1 to 6, of the Kronsfeld School in the village of Haskett in southern Manitoba. He was much older than the teen-aged permit holders they were accustomed to; stoop-shouldered, tall and gaunt, with reddish hair, sallow complexion, a large nose, and protruding ears, he was a formidable figure. He signed himself Fred Grove.[1]

He had been sent there by Andrew Weidenhammer, whose inspectorate took in all of the German-English bilingual schools of the Mennonite Reserve, on the recommendation of Robert Fletcher, deputy minister of Education, with whom Grove had had an interview in Winnipeg. As Fletcher told the story, a man calling himself Grove had phoned his office asking for an interview, which had been arranged, but shortly he phoned again saying that he didn't know whether it would make any difference, but he had only the clothes he stood up in—overalls and a workshirt. Fletcher said that he often wore those clothes himself and that they would not affect job prospects.

Indeed, Grove must have been a welcome sight to the deputy minister. Here was a mature man, obviously intelligent, with evident teaching experience, and he spoke both German and English, even though his English had a marked European sound. At the time, Manitoba had an ambitious and idealistic bilingual school system, developing out of the French-English background of the province, but extended to bilingual schools for the settlements of Polish, Ruthenian, Swedish, Austrian, Icelandic, and German newcomers, to try to help them in the transition to their adopted country. Staffing the bilingual schools was a constant problem.

Within this system, Weidenhammer's inspectorate—in which there were seventy-five schools by the time Grove arrived—had

YEARY LIBRARY
LAREDO JR. COLLEGE
LAREDO, TEXAS

a special distinction as being concerned not only with a particular language group, but also with a particular religious group. The Canadian government had made definite commitments to the nearly seven thousand Mennonites who, in the 1870's, came from southern Russia, and who "had behind them on their arrival in Manitoba a three-and-one-half centuries long agrarian and pioneering tradition which they had carried as freemen from the hearth of their origins in the Low Countries to the Baltic marshes of Prussia and Poland and thence through four generations on the open steppes of South Russia." [2] These very desirable settlers were given rich farmland in the Red River valley, and they were promised ethnically homogeneous settlements, exemption from military service, and the right to keep German as the language of instruction in their schools. It was not only an intelligent practice; it was an obligation to provide them with German-speaking teachers. It is not at all unlikely that Grove went to Manitoba because he knew of the Mennonite settlement and the bilingual schools there.

In these schools there were already a number of teachers who were newly arrived foreigners, eagerly hired by the Department of Education because they were German speakers. They had been educated in Russia, in the United States, in Austria, and in various parts of Germany. One man who was teaching on a permit claimed to have received his education in "Germany, France, England, Scotland, and Canada"; another had a note by his name, "Certificates lost by fire." [3] Grove's was not an unusual case, nor were his claims unusual. Neither was the deputy minister making any deep commitment to the stranger in overalls when he sent him to the one-room school in Haskett.

As villages went, Haskett was busier than most. Only three miles north of the Manitoba-Dakota border, it was a port of entry on the Great Northern Railway, and so it had a customs and immigration house in addition to the station, and it had three trains a day: one passenger train up to Winnipeg, one passenger train down to the United States, and a freight train either way. It had three stores, two lumberyards, machine shops, livery stables, and two elevators. Around it, to the east and north, stretched the great plain of ancient Lake Agassiz, while close by were the Pembina Hills—mountains, some called them.

The whole district was well established, prospering—and divided. The little white one-room schoolhouse was a symbol of that division. Its name was that of its original site three miles away at Kronsfeld, from which it had been moved because the majority of the people there were ultraconservative "Old Colony" Mennonites who were bitterly opposed to the public schools, which they regarded as a threat to their faith and a breach of the government's promises. They supported and sent their children to a rival, church-run school in which all instruction was in German. As a result, in this quite populous area, there were only twenty children in the school in Haskett. Yet the fact that nearly all of the teachers in the public schools throughout the reserve were Mennonites—children and grandchildren of the original settlers—showed that the Old Colony views, the authority of the church, and within families the patriarchal rule were being challenged. There was a strong transitional movement under way.

It is a remarkable thing that, while Grove did set one novel, *Fruits of the Earth,* in this physical area, nowhere did he overtly portray the Mennonite community, its culture, nor its divisions. It is equally remarkable that one of his most persistent themes is the generation conflict, and in particular the defying of patriarchal authority—this in spite of the fact that the patriarchal concept is foreign to the general movement of the New World and notably to that of western Canada. Only in special religious communities such as the Mennonite Reserve was the breakdown of patriarchal rule a question of vital moment. Perhaps that is why *Our Daily Bread,* which Grove did base on a Mennonite family, his wife's family, seems remote and staged.

Meanwhile, in the Kronsfeld school, Grove had a job to do, and the attendance record, in his meticulous handwriting, gives the schedule of his work week by week. In German there was translation, dictation, grammar, reading of "Der Heimat," and "Der Wohnort," and verses for grade-oners to memorize—"Der Fuchs und Die Gans" was one of them. Other subjects were in English: history, the origins of Great Britain up to 1066; geography, a study of Canada and adjoining states of the United States; arithmetic; readings about Canada, Canadian timber, the sawmill, Chinook winds, the coyote. And then elementary science and nature study: lessons on the pulley and the lever, observation of the stars and phases of the moon, elements of plant life, including trees of the neighborhood. In May, under nature study, the dandelion; under science, growing beans in pots.

Outside the school, there are many memories of him. He was welcome in the homes of his pupils where he often dropped in "to get the good German food" and to play with the children: "Oh I admired the long slim fellow who stepped with one step into the buggy!" "Our parents welcomed him because he was a teacher and a teacher was highly respected in those days." But at the same time he was puzzling. He would not kill anything, anything at all. If he found a half-frozen mouse he would take it into his room till it revived. When the wolves came howling down from the Pembina Hills, he fed them. He *fed* the wolves. "Oh he was a strange man. We never quite understood him, but we greatly admired him." Or again, "He was queer. Besides that, he was German, you know; *echt Deutsch*—real German." [4]

The strangest thing—and one that was talked about for many years—was what happened at the school picnic in June, shortly before Grove left; Jake Giesbrecht, who was a special pupil of Grove's, was there. Jake was sixteen and he could not go to school in the daytime because he was doing a man's work on the farm, but for a couple of months during the winter he had ridden in at night to take grade 8 work from Grove. He was one of the boys whom Grove characterized as Len in *The Yoke of Life,* boys who exemplified for him Rousseau's theme of unequal opportunities, a theme with particular fascination for Grove. The two of them sat in the lean-to that had been added to the school for the teacher to live in; it was littered with plants and papers, insects, and an occasional mouse; and on the table was a large glass bowl filled with tobacco for Grove's roll-your-own chain smoking. They became good friends. And so for the picnic, Jake drove a wagon-load of teacher and pupils to a picnic site in a steep ravine in the Pembina Hills. After they got there,

Well I was busy unhitching the horses, and I find out there's a commotion going on. The boys had found a nest of snakes, you know, the school boys. And they started to kill them. And before I knew what's happening, Mr. Grove stands right in the middle of that nest and he says, "Before you kill another snake, you kill me!"

Well! What's the man talking about? A snake—had to be killed, you know. With us—a snake—from the Bible, you know? What didn't the snake do, yes? The old ideas about it, you know. And he said, "Before you kill another snake you kill me!" And those boys—they didn't kill another snake.

The idea was this—transmigration? He figured that some day his soul might go into a snake. He hadn't told me about that idea of transmigration before that. I couldn't grasp it. That was something new to me.[5]

The talk of transmigration alarmed the Mennonite elders; this man was certainly not one of them.

The six months at Haskett gave Grove a time of respite, a chance to gather himself together, to feel his way out from this little haven, to gain some knowledge of the country—as well as of British history—and to prepare a solid base of official standing in the teaching profession. To that end, in June he took the provincial teachers' examination in grade 12 mathematics and history, which constituted half of the requirements for the first-class certificate, then attended Weidenhammer's ten-week normal school for bilingual teachers, and by the end of the summer he was no longer teaching on a permit; he had professional standing.

It was not until Weidenhammer announced the appointments in his inspectorate at the closing exercises of the normal school that Grove's position as the new principal of the Winkler Intermediate School became official, but the school board had agreed to take him, and the appointment had been reported in the newspaper at the beginning of June. The board had accepted him upon the urging of their departing principal, I. J. Warkentin, a young Mennonite of twenty-six, who, having his bachelor's degree from the University of Manitoba, was going to Germany to do graduate work at Leipzig. His uncle was one of Grove's supporters at Haskett. He had met Grove there and had discovered in the older man a keenness like his own for teaching, an eagerness for new methods, new devices, new texts, and new educational theories: "There were so many things in the air at that time: playground facilities, manual training, visual education, new arithmetic and so forth." [6] He was satisfied that Grove would make a good leader for the school. As for Grove, the principalship of the two-story, four-room brick school at Winkler was a great advance over his lonely post fifteen miles south. The town had a population of well over six hundred, and according to the inspector's report there were nearly 160 pupils in the school: 111

Mennonites, 29 Germans, 15 Jews, 3 English. The principal's salary was $1,000 a year.

Together with the large number of Mennonite pupils in the school, the fact that the other three teachers were all Mennonites showed that the Old Colony was not strong here. Tena Wiens, the primary teacher, and John Enns, in charge of room II—and at whose home Grove lived—were both in their early twenties, both Canadians born in the reserve. The other teacher was different. He was close to Grove's own age; he had been born and partly educated in southern Russia; he had been teaching for close to twenty years, fifteen of them in church-run schools; and he was deeply religious. The two men did not care for each other.

Grove began boldly with lengthy notices in *The Morden Times*. The first was aimed at increasing enrollment in high school grades and at helping teachers in nearby rural schools to get advanced standing: "The courses will comprise all grades of the public school programme and the bi-lingual teachers' course, grades IX and X. If a sufficient attendance can be secured there will also be a special teachers' course in the evening, comprising the work for full third and second classes (grades X and XI) . . ." (July 31). The second notice, even more ambitious, was aimed both at involving the community as a whole, and at getting funds for school equipment:

The entrance class (grade 8) of the Winkler Intermediate School issues the following preliminary announcement. Under the strict supervision and responsibility of the principal they will carry on seed tests for farm seeds, grain as well as garden truck etc. The seeds will be tested as to purity, quality and percentage of germination. Farmers in the Southern part of Manitoba are invited to take advantage of this opportunity. . . . There will be no charge for these tests, but if those who wish to take advantage of this offer choose to contribute a few cents toward the equipment fund of the school, their names will be recorded in a book provided for this purpose. . . . (September 11, 1913)

It was a long way from growing beans in pots, and no one could accuse Grove of petty planning, but apparently he was not aware that in this country the Department of Agriculture had done such testing for a number of years, and without hinting at a silver collection.

That fall it was Winkler's turn to be host to to the Annual Conference of the German-English Teachers of Southern Manitoba, and Grove had to help in preparations for that. The custom of these conferences—this was the thirteenth—was to have the proceedings of the first day conducted in German, so that the entire community could understand and take part, and the second day's proceedings in English. It was also customary on the afternoon of the first (German) day to have one paper on educational theory or philosophy, and another on educational method or practice. On this occasion, a teacher from a neighboring town, an American Mennonite trained in the United States, spoke on the nineteenth-century German philosopher and educator, Johann Herbart, and Grove gave a paper on elementary education in Germany.

There is a vivid glimpse of these busy months in the letters that Grove wrote to young Warkentin, now a graduate student at Leipzig.[7] The first letters are lively, full of plans; he is enjoying the stir that he is making. He asks for books—books on new methods of teaching mathematics, but especially for the eight volumes of Rein-Pickel's *Volksschulunterricht* (Leipzig, 1889) which was a completely described curriculum for German elementary schools. He was buying telescopes, setting up physics equipment, starting a wood-working class, gathering moths, caterpillars, beetles, frogs, and reorganizing the classrooms so that by November he was teaching only high school grades. He also demoted students who had been advanced too quickly, a move that was probably intended to annoy his second in command, and did: "P. H. is mad. He thinks I am the most interfering fellow he has ever met with." One thing that these letters establish beyond question is that whatever else Grove may have been, he was a professional and professionally trained elementary school teacher before he arrived in Manitoba.

But by December, the self-confident tone has gone. There had been an open break with P. H., and some of the trustees sided with him. Grove won the argument, but "I am bleeding." As he lists all the things he has done and all the grievances he has, the tone becomes curiously adolescent. There is no sense of proportion or relative values—or of humor. Instead there is a note of panic—"*I have got* to win out," the words heavily underlined—

which opens up vistas of past failures and sets the Winkler venture in quite a new light.

At the end of the December letter a note is tacked on: "Did I tell you that I am going to get married soon?" There is not another letter until February, and it is full of despair. The young woman whom he had expected to marry had turned him away, and his world was shattered: "At Christmas I went down to Arkansas—into the hospital!! And when I came out, after a week of raving fever, I did not know my world any longer! It was so changed."

Things have got worse in the school; his training and experience are disregarded. He is an outsider: "they listen to the talk of a disgruntled man *who belongs to them.*" He is rejected: "I'd stay if they wanted me to . . . but they don't." "There ought to be a school somewhere that *suits* me." The gloom is thick. "In the whole of life I do not see any sense. . . . My love for dogs, pups and all kinds of animals rests in the firm conviction that their life is the only sincere, the only untainted life." He longs to become a recluse in a little place near Etaples on the French coast, "to live there in absolute seclusion, write a poem now and then and finish a book that I have been working on between times for 20 years." In these pages is the kernel of the first part of *In Search of Myself,* including the Swedish father, the Scotch mother, the seduction by an older woman, her subsequent divorce, and so on. As his sense of injury deepens—"the way I'm treated here"—so his claims to learning, to travel, even to sophistication grow more exaggerated. The letters give an extraordinary view of a tense, driven, volatile, vulnerable man.

But the despair did not last. The school board did invite him back for a second year, and Grove did find sympathy and warmth from some of the younger people, especially two of his teacher-students, John Enns and Abram Kroeker. Kroeker recalled, "He was older than John and me, a lot older; at the same time we were friends—not just students and instructor—we were friends. When Easter time came and the teachers' convention in Winnipeg, he said to us, 'John and Abe, I want you to have dinner with me at the C.N.R. hotel, because we'll all be in Winnipeg.' And so I know that his favorite dish was stuffed peppers!" And he went on, "I think John and I loved him. I think it was love." [8]

Grove found comfort and affection from another person too,

from Tena Wiens, the primary teacher. Some felt that she should not marry him because he was too old for her; others felt that he should have a city-bred wife. But Fred Grove and Tena Wiens went their own way. In July, after Grove had finished marking grade 8 provincial examinations, he went to join Tena at her home in Rush Lake, Saskatchewan, the short-grass country of *Our Daily Bread,* where her family had moved from the reserve a few years before. They were married in the Anglican church in Swift Current on August 2, 1914. According to the marriage certificate, the bride was Tena Wiens, age twenty-two, born in Plum Coulee, Manitoba.

The groom: Frederick Philip Grove, age 41
Birthplace: Moscow
Marital status: Widower
Parents: Charles Edward Grove and Bertha Rutherford Grove
Occupation: Professor of Science (Scholastic)
Religious denomination: Lutheran.

Shortly they returned to Winkler where they rented rooms above the hardware store, and both continued to teach for the next school year.

Meantime, the war had broken out. The Mennonites, of course, were pacifists, but very quickly rifts appeared among the school's pupils between the passionately Canadian Mennonites and the small group of Germans. As he often did, Grove gave his support to the minority. Entering the classroom one day when the students were quarreling over the war, he said, "Who's for Germany?" One of the German girls put up her hand, presently a boy put up his. Grove said, "Then it is the three of us against the world!" Inside and outside the school, he continued to praise, as he had always done, German science, German literature, German music, and German education. It was a courageous and salutary stand to take. Except that he then complained that people in the town—a Dr. Weatherhead among them—were spreading rumors that he was pro-German.

The strange naïveté of his complaints was a continuing trait with Grove. Fully predictable human reactions to his views or conduct were always a surprise to him, Grove feeling virtuous in his own intent and unaware of the possibility of other viewpoints—or at least of other viewpoints worth considering. The same thing is true of his complaints of being shut out by the community. Winkler was a religious town, but Grove did not go to church—not to any church. Neither did he conduct religious exercises within the school that were allowed by law and that the other teachers did conduct. On the other hand, he did encourage students to question Mennonite doctrine. Where religion was concerned, he was quite as self-righteous and uncompromising as any Old Colony Mennonite.

In general, the townsfolk of Winkler found Grove overbearing. He was too impatient with the school board, too arrogant in manner: *"Er arbeitet zu sehr von oben herab"* (he works too much from the top down) was the way the older people put it. "Now we Mennonites, amongst ourselves, do not like to be bossed, whereas Grove was used to ordering and bossing things. And so trouble followed." [9] Grove was not invited to stay for a third year. He had failed in the ambitious plans with which he began, and he had failed largely because of his lack of interest in other people, in their views or their sensitivities, a lack that amounted to stupidity.

Yet those who were his students—and there is a surprising number of them yet living—remember his teaching vividly and with gratitude, especially the classes in nature study. They remember, too, the yarns he told. When he taught history or geography, he had always been at the place. He was with the German ambassadorial service in Greece digging for artifacts when the house they were staying in collapsed, undermined by hogs rooting at night. In his first night at a new school in Montana he was awakened at five in the morning by a child saying, "Mamma wants to set the table and you're sleeping on the table cloth." When he was with the German consulate in London, he happened to collide with a fashionable lady who cursed him in the language of a street cleaner. When he was a tobacco farmer in Kentucky he sewed on the ear of his wife that had been bitten off by one of their favorite Percherons. One former pupil said, "There was never a dull day at school with Mr. Grove"; another, "He was a great teller of tales."

The story of his former wife went with further hints about the other family of this "widower," who had one son—or more—figures as shadowy as the five that Rousseau placed in foundling hospitals. They were part of the air of mystery that Grove liked to encourage about himself, as on the occasion when he told a young man who met him only the once, and then only for a short hour, that his name was not Grove but Gropfe.

Both Mennonites and Germans in the community took it for granted that Grove was German, and some of those closest to him thought that he had recently come over from Germany. The general impression was expressed by Ben Warkentin, now a retired school inspector, then the young man who knew Grove for that one short hour, who recalled him pacing up and down, chain smoking, a man filled with anxiety, urgency, "a mind detached from his environment, a spirit but slightly affected by his varied contact with his fellow-man, he became part of his creation—and the Canadian knew him to be an out-lander." [10]

CHAPTER 2

"Rousseau as Educator"

I N THE fall of 1914 while he was at Winkler, Grove published two articles, one in English and one in German, both on education. They are the earliest work of his published in Canada that is known, and they are important in that they reveal the frame of reference of Grove's thinking—nineteenth-century German educational theory, developing from the Rousseau-Pestalozzi-Froebel-Herbart chain of ideas.

The first article, in the form of a letter to the editor of *The Western School Journal*,[1] is about his experience in July in marking the departmental grade 8 examinations in grammar and geometry, which were the two papers to which he was assigned. It is the work of a trained, intelligent, and concerned schoolteacher who has an educational philosophy. He deplores the hopeless floundering of the students among grammatical terms which they do not understand and their attempts at logical proofs which are beyond the capacities of their age group. He suggests that the objectives of the courses have not been made clear to the teachers themselves, and he recommends compilation of a detailed syllabus for their guidance such as that "prepared by the authorities of the city of Hamburg for the guidance of her public school teachers. It comprises all the grades and all the subjects—it is a normal school course within the brief compass of about sixty pages."

His deepest concern, however, is for two fundamental and interlocking concepts of the nature of education: learning through discovery, and "cultural epochs." Geometry, for instance, should be a severely practical course in constructive drawing at this stage, whereby children would discover "a necessary link between arithmetic and deductive mathematics." But this purpose was defeated. "It seemed as if immature teachers had been trying to show their newly acquired knowledge to their classes, instead of

skilfully leading the children into a field of triumphant discoveries
—the first they approach, and one that, rightly led, they will approach with enthusiasm, zeal and the satisfaction of conquerors."
Moreover, to guide the steps of these discoveries, there is a kind
of ordained syllabus in the history of the race. Here the educational theories merged with biological theories of evolution and
with anthropological theories of the phases of human development in the cultural epochs of Herbart. Just as the frog or the
butterfly goes through all the stages of development of its race,
so a child passes through all stages of human development. As
Grove puts it, "This procedure has been the procedure of the race,
and it is well that it should be the procedure of the child mind."
Education so based will be education according to nature, regenerative and indestructible. There was such widespread excitement about these ideas that one English educator declared,
"Fröbel and Herbart are probably the two men who will dominate
sound education for the next 300 years." [2]

The nucleus of this educational process was nature study and
mathematics, the basic combination of the Froebelian system.
Nature study was not only to develop alert observation but to
lead the child to discover the essential unity and harmony of
all created things. It would provide a kind of religion. Mathematics must accompany nature study so that the child could discover the laws of nature—its discipline—for nature is not chaos.
Froebel's pantheism and Wordsworth's were very close.

It is this complex of ideas that explains what at first seems
surprising about Grove—that he was primarily and especially a
teacher of natural science and of mathematics. When he described himself rather pompously on his marriage certificate as
"Professor of Science," he meant it. And of course the concept
of the unity of nature was at the bottom of his championing of
snakes and so forth. He was less a Hindu than a Romantic. In
his novels, this background appears in the importance of the
theme of metamorphosis, in the ceaseless concern with shifting
cultural epochs, in his various attempts to portray the whole
history of man, as well as in his meticulous accounting of miles
and hours and bushels and trees.

Grove expands these ideas in his article on "Rousseau as Educator," which was published in successive issues of the German-
language newspaper, *Der Nordwesten*.[3] It was the text of the

talk Grove gave at the 1914 Bi-lingual Teachers' Conference held in the village of Plum Coulee, his bride's birthplace. The tone of this article is less engaging than the one on examinations; there is a tendency to condescension which is accompanied by a pretentiousness that appears often in Grove. On this occasion, Grove chides commentators who read "not Rousseau, but rather criticisms of him or excerpts from his books," a remark that does not come gracefully from one who is himself using an English translation of *Emile* that is abridged to half the length of Rousseau's original.[4] Even less attractive is Grove's citing of "the views of some of Rousseau's prominent fellow countrymen," as if from firsthand knowledge, though his quotations are all taken from the appendix of the abridged translation. He also makes free and unacknowledged use of the editor's preface and the translator's introduction; in fact, some of his most telling remarks come from their pages.

As the editor says and Grove reiterates: "Without a study of the *Emile* one can not explain Pestalozzi, Basedow, Froebel, or any of the great leaders in education that belong to the present century (xvi)." We might paraphrase that statement to read that without a study of the *Emile, The Social Contract,* and *The Origin of Inequality* we cannot explain a great part of Grove's writings. Just as he pointed out that the *Emile* is not systematic argument, but rather a romance, we might also note that much of his writing is fictionalized applications of Rousseau's tenets. In this paper, Grove presented views and convictions that were fundamental to most of his writing, and it provides an insight into the essential composition of his intellectual equipment, which by this time had been set and which changed very little within the following thirty years. It is worth repeating that these views and convictions are contained within the framework of nineteenth-century German theory about elementary education and that that is the body of reference and learning that is pertinent to the background of Grove's work.

The opening of *Emile*—"Everything is good as it comes from the hands of the Author of Nature; but everything degenerates in the hands of men"—is of course Grove's starting point in this article when he propounds Rousseau's views of a redemptive education which will create a renewed man, win him back, through a direct observation of nature and her laws, from the distorting influence of books, will restore his original goodness intended by a beneficent nature, will assert the supremacy of the individual as a whole being over the citizen who is only a fragment, and will sweep away the power structure of class society which has brought about man's degeneration. The theme of degenerative society and the cleansing power of nature is the movement of *The Yoke of Life* as it is the overall pattern of *A Search for America*.

The beginning of that society lies in the paradox of man who is created an individual but who, in order to survive, needs help which he gets through the family, the first form of society, and itself, Grove says, "the nucleus of nations." This idea is the informing impetus of the trilogy about the degeneration of the family, beginning with the story of the patriarch John Elliot in *Our Daily Bread*. The family chaos is the symbol of the chaos of nations; society—or the family—is taking the wrong turn.

To redress the degenerative influence of society, as Grove says, "Rousseau's education is intended as education for individuality," and the aim of Emile's tutor is "to educate this one boy to be a man." Such also is the aim of the saintly school teacher in *The Yoke of Life*. But the deep structure that is involved here is the essence of the individual—the "I, Myself," the "permanent substratum"—which obeys and must obey its own laws and directions because otherwise it would be denying itself. This concept Grove took to himself as a justification of his, at times, extraordinary perverseness and callousness; and he applies it to his characters—to Mrs. Vogel of *Settlers*, or Edmund of *The Master of the Mill*, for instance—who could not act otherwise than according to the laws of their own nature. Within that reference, they are justified. It is society that has misdirected them. This notion explains to some degree why there is so very little shading in Grove's character portrayals, for these individuals are absolutes that cannot be questioned.

Moreover, like nature, "the natural man is perfect in himself," he is "the absolute whole," whereas the citizen is fractured, only a part of a whole. Education, according to Rousseau, can produce a man or a citizen, but not both. Rousseau's sharp division became for Grove a rigorous dichotomy and is the basis of his own declaration in the 1913-14 letters that he could never be a citizen or a burgher. It is also the basis of his antagonism to civilization, the city, and its complements—even when taking advantage of their amenities. Consistency never bothered Grove.

Education of the individual must progress according to the individual's growth, according to "nature." Grove summarizes Rousseau's four stages of development—later elaborated upon in the Herbartian "culture epochs"—and quotes and repeats with great emphasis: "Allow the essence of childhood to reach maturity!" This admirable dictum of Rousseau's is the ground for Grove's opposition to teaching a child to read and write, which opposition, he says, "is a growing movement from the German schools of the Herbartians." There should be, instead, a training of the senses—"Our first teachers of philosophy are our feet, hands and eyes"—which will awaken in the child a desire for knowledge so that he will discover for himself the laws of nature or science and so teach his tutor. This training of the senses can be gained through the Froebelian methods of play, for "a child thinks with its muscles." Lecturing and verbalism in general on the part of the teacher should be prohibited; direct instruction should be postponed as long as possible. This argument helps to explain what at times seems to be a strange contradiction in Grove between his scorn of books and "book learning" and his own avid reading, as though he had been starved for books.

Then there are Rousseau's negatives: "Don't save time; lose it," that is, do not push the child; "Don't awaken evil by preaching good," for there is no original sin in the human heart. The child has his own morality, and since man is innately good, he can only be harmed by having outside impressions forced upon him. Nevertheless, of course, the child needs the guidance and sympathy of the teacher, and Grove assures his audience that "Rousseau knows no bounds when he talks of the sacredness, the responsibility of the teaching profession."

Rousseau's ideas are repeated over and over again in Grove's lectures, in his articles, and in his books. A great part of the unconvincing nature of the true lovers in *Settlers*, for instance, stems from *Emile*. In Niels and Ellen, Grove reproduces Emile and Sophie, who were only figurines to begin with, and puts them through additional theoretical moves. It's worth noting that neither Rousseau nor Grove seems to know what to do with Emile when he grows up, how to get him over what apparently to them was the overwhelming hurdle from adolescence to maturity, nor how to recognize sex as a not uncommon part of life. This may be the cause of the arrested development that afflicts most of Grove's men; and what seems to be a rigid Calvinism in him may simply be another compliment to his master, Rousseau.

At any rate, the educational theories in these two articles, which had been first established on this continent in Pennsylvania and New York, had been sweeping the United States with a fervor similar to Grove's. It was paradoxical that he should advocate them, of all areas on the continent, within the singularly conservative cultural tradition of the Mennonites. On the other hand, to inveigh against luxury among these plain-living people, to advocate the salutary need for manual training for children whose few hours in school were the only ones saved from manual work, to lecture against "book learning" to those who rarely owned a book, to advocate a return to firsthand observation of nature to those who saw little else—in other words, to apply the theories which had been based on a sophisticated city-bred society as educational articles of faith shows in some measure Grove's own lack of adaptability, his inability to observe or comprehend human nature around him, however keen his eyes might be for the details of flower or bird.

CHAPTER 3

Town and Country

IN THE next seven years, after he left Winkler, Grove taught in six different schools, and in one of them for two separate stints. Within one nine-month period he taught in three schools, a record that he later attributed to the aimless elder son of "The Weatherhead Fortunes."

First he went about two hundred miles west across the plain to teach in the high school at Virden, a town of about two thousand, three times the size of Winkler, which had sprung up with the coming of the Canadian Pacific Railroad in 1882, and whose townspeople were chiefly from Ontario and the British Isles. Virden was particularly proud of its educational record and of its two fine brick schools, the public school with a staff of nine, the collegiate with a staff of four, and a combined enrollment of about 450. Fifteen Virden young people were attending university in 1915 and holding their own in scholarships.[1]

Grove's three colleagues in the high school all held bachelor of arts degrees from the University of Toronto. The principal, who was about to retire, had an honors degree in English and history; Miss Gilray held an honors degree in modern languages; and Mr. Anderson, a recent graduate, had his degree in science. He and Grove were both newcomers, their predecessors having enlisted in the army. Anderson taught the sciences, and Grove had been hired to teach mathematics. His salary was $1,400 for the year, which was less than he and his wife had earned together in the previous year at Winkler but was still a very respectable salary; the principal got only $1,700.

The Groves moved to Virden in July to take advantage of the hospital there, where their daughter, Phyllis May, was born on August 5, 1915. In September, Grove resumed his pursuit of academic credit and so of higher professional standing. He applied for and was granted admission to the University of Mani-

toba as an extramural student,[2] but he first had to complete the
grade 12 or first year university course, of which he had taken
Part I two years before. At the time, grade 12 and first year were
equivalents, the university first year being a convenience for
students in areas where there was no grade 12. University work
proper began only with second year, which would now be the
freshman year.

The student card for Frederick Philip Grove, age forty-two, of
Virden, Manitoba, has a note which reads: "Was allowed to enter
upon First Year work and granted exemption from Mathematics."
By Christmas there is another note: "Owing to creditable showing in 1st term work, was allowed to take entire 2nd year exam
in April, 1916." His results in these April examinations for what
would now be a freshman university course are worth noting
because they show his areas of strength (first-class or A standing
is 80 percent or over), and so the obvious reason for his major-
ing in German and French. They also show areas in which he
had no particular distinction even at this elementary level—Latin
grammar, Latin authors, logic—areas in which he later made ex-
pansive claims to learning at various times. It is less surprising
that he did not do well in English literature and composition nor
in English history, although he had been teaching high school
courses in these subjects for two years.

Hist. of Lit. & Verse	56%
Prose Lit. & Comp.	48
Logic	68
Political Economy	55
Latin Grammar	74
Latin Authors	68
History	59
French Grammar	83
French Authors	78
German Grammar	100
German Authors	92

In the same year, Mrs. Grove, who had taken her grade 10 and
grade 11 work under her husband's tutelage, wrote and passed
her grade 11 exams in June 1916.[3] Evidently, plans were going
ahead for both of them as professional teachers for future years.

No wonder that Virden people saw a light in the Groves' house at all hours of the night and wondered if they ever slept.

For various reasons, the year at Virden was not a happy experience either for Grove or for those who had dealings with him. The intensive study that he was doing on top of his teaching, and the exciting but disturbing presence of the baby May were enough to put some strain on the most equable nature, and Grove's was not that. But much more seriously, toward the end of January he came down with a severe case of pneumonia, and a substitute teacher had to take over his classes for several weeks. Later he used the experience of this most depressing illness with its hallucinatory delirium in several novels, most notably in *A Search for America* and *The Yoke of Life*. The immediate effect was to fill him with anxiety, with fear of a long illness which could destroy professional and financial security, and it added to his general tendency toward hypochondria and money-mindedness.

Across the street from the Groves' two-story frame house was the Scarth family. Mrs. Scarth, who had been a nurse, had already been concerned about the young Mrs. Grove and her baby. During the worst of Grove's illness, she took charge and helped to nurse him; her five-year-old daughter carried hot dishes to him, and her thirteen-year-old son cut and split wood and did any other necessary household chores. He recalls that "on somewhat rare occasions Grove would smile and be pleasant and co-operative," but his mother found him "not a pleasant personality, nor considerate"; yet "Mr. Grove was a human being in trouble," and she went to him.[4]

Among the teachers—and there are three left who knew him there—there is a common recollection that Grove was "an odd man," inclined to tell strange tales about himself—"fact and fancy to him were pretty well the same thing"—and among the tales were those of a shadowy first family with two or three sons— "he seemed to be very vague in his mind regarding how many there were"—all of them in different universities, one at Yale.[5] As for those who were his students in that year, there is among them none of the sense of companionship that some Winkler students had. Rather, there are recollections of an impatient man given to violent outbursts of temper and to wounding sarcasm.

There are some bitter memories. There was little regret on either side when Grove left Virden.

On Thursday, August 10, 1916, *The Gladstone Age* announced: "Mr. Grove of Virden who has been engaged as Principal of Gladstone School has arrived in town with his family and taken up residence in the suite over the Drug Store." Gladstone was small, about the size of Winkler, but it was one of the older settlements in Manitoba. The people were chiefly of Scotch descent, though there was a fair admixture from the rest of the British Isles, and their loyalties were evident in the town's name. It appears in Grove's books as "Balfour," the name of another British prime minister.

The school was one of the early ones in the province as the number of the school district, 70, shows—even Virden was 144— but it was only three years before, in 1913, that Gladstone had achieved high school status. In practical terms that meant that two of the six rooms in the brick building were set aside for grades 9, 10, and 11. Still, Grove had fulfilled one ambition; he was at last a high school principal. The other high school teacher was Miss McManus, who held a master's degree from New Brunswick, who taught French, Latin, literature, British and Canadian history, and civics. Grove as usual taught mathematics and the sciences—chemistry, physics, and nature study. The two did not like each other. There were 64 students in the high school out of a total enrollment of 229, and Grove's salary was the same as that at Virden, $1,400. This opening also had come about because his predecessor had joined the army.

Memories in Gladstone are of Grove's aloofness—"He was never a friendly man in town here"; of his dourness—"I can honestly say that I never heard that man laugh, and I don't believe I ever saw him smile in the classroom or outside"; and of his impatience with those who were slow to learn. And of one other thing —his insistence that he had not been born in Russia, but in Kurland. "He told us that in school many times. It was sort of an obsession with him. This occupied a very prominent part of his thinking, that he wanted to impress on us that he was a Kurlander. It wasn't pride of country at all; it was a sort of defensive thing." [6] As for Grove's claim that he had championed an unjustly used Anglican clergyman in Gladstone, the claim was stoutly countered when it appeared in *In Search of Myself*, by

knowledgeable Anglicans who said that Grove was not an Anglican, that he rarely went to church, that he was not a member of
the congregation, and that he was never involved in any matter of
congregational policy.

During the school year, he did continue with his university
work extramurally, and by this stage, as a major student, he was
taking courses in only French and German. There were few
majors in either department in Grove's year: 7 in French, of whom
two got A standing; 5 in German, of whom three got A standing.[7] When the results came out in May, Fred P. Grove had the
first scholarship in French of $150 (which was paid him); [8] he
also had won "First Scholarship. Hon. Mention" in German,
though the money for the scholarship reverted to the next student, who also had A standing—a practice still commonly followed in many universities to divide up scholarship funds.
Grove's memory deceived him when he wrote in *In Search of
Myself:* "payments of the amounts being conditional upon attendance at the university, I forfeited both to the next in line"
(295).

As his student card notes, he applied for and was given permission to write his full fourth-year examinations the following
September. The chairmen of both departments, as well as the
University Board of Studies, were doing everything in their
power to help Grove, but he made an abrupt and unexplained
shift in plans. He did not write his fourth-year examinations in
September; in fact, he left his university work altogether and did
not return to it for four years.

Instead of spending the summer of 1917 in study, both of the
Groves took schools in rural communities: Mrs. Grove at Falmouth, a newly built school in a German settlement some forty
miles northeast of Gladstone; and Grove at Leifur, an older
school twenty-five miles beyond that, for the two summer months.
There he boarded with a farmer and on weekends bicycled to
Falmouth where Mrs. Grove and little May were living in the
teacherage. These trips he wrote about in *The Turn of the Year,*
and the Leifur area with the lake a couple of miles away also
appears in the latter part of *The Yoke of Life.*

On August 30, *The Gladstone Age* noted, "Mr. F.W. [*sic*]
Grove returned to town this week to resume his position as Principal of the school." That is the last time that the paper mentions

Grove's name, an indication of a growing coolness toward him that seems to have increased when the high school results turned out to be disappointing. The high school enrollment dropped sharply from 64 to 41.[9] It is not difficult to imagine exchanges between Grove and the school board becoming increasingly acid until, at their January meeting, the secretary read a letter "from Mr. Grove tendering his resignation as Principal to take effect 1st March or earlier." They accepted his resignation and engaged another teacher at a higher salary. By March 1, 1918, Grove was teaching at Ferguson school, four and a half miles from Mrs. Grove, within the same German settlement, and was living with his family in the Falmouth teacherage. It was the trips that he made to and from Falmouth from September until he left Gladstone in mid-term that were the subject of *Over Prairie Trails*.

During those few months, Mrs. Grove and two-year-old May had been watched over by a solicitous and grateful though widespread community. During the day, the 28 pupils, ranging in age from five to thirteen, provided plenty of company, the girls vied for the honor of looking after teacher's golden-haired little girl, and the boys brought the eggs, milk, meat, and other supplies that Mrs. Grove bought from her nearby neighbors—nearby meaning a mile off.

In the two one-room schools of Falmouth and Ferguson, in the Big Grassy Marsh country where many of the children spoke not a word of English, the Groves, with their training and their language background, were a godsend. There is no mention of them in any of the newspapers of the surrounding area, which is understandable, for there would be only the rare person in either school district who could write English, and none with the time or interest to be a local correspondent. But perhaps because, knowing no English, the people of the settlement had little contact with the outside world, because they were turned in upon themselves, the memory of those years is the keener among the surprising number of Grove pupils still living in the area, the children of *Settlers of the Marsh* and *The Yoke of Life:* [10]

Edward Elke: Our family was seven children and our father and mother. They went to town once a year, in the fall, to buy a few clothes and shoes and things. The fathers were shoemakers and the mothers were dressmakers, and what was too small for the big one was remodelled and made for the little one.

It was the school's first day of school. That's when Mrs. Grove opened up. We lived a mile north of Falmouth school. Never forget wading through the swamp the first trip. My older sister and brother, they were taller than I was so they had to lift me through. That's the way I started school.

Lydia Campbell: Half a mile west and about half a mile south, we were. Then there were no fences, you see, it was mostly bush and we just took off from home and went straight across to the school. It was homestead land at that time, and it was a homestead my dad had taken, and that's how come we were living there.

Roy Oswald: We were four miles from school, actually over four miles and that was quite a walk. Sometimes we missed in the winter time.

Arthur Lange: The Department of Education—I guess they sent them out because they knew that it was a German settlement.

Rudolph Elke: We were all German people, you see, and we could hardly talk English. And I think that was one reason she came there. Because the whole community was mostly German, you see. And when there was recess or something like that, there was nothing but German going on.

Lydia Elke: She had to teach us the English. She'd say, Well then, what's this? and what's this? and this? So when she came to the nose, none of us knew what it was, and this Daisy Epp she quick put her hand up—Well, what is it? Nais, she said.

Lydia Campbell: I think my cousins and my brothers and I were the only English speaking children. We learned a good many German words.

Little May used to play around the door of the school and quietly come in. She never made a disturbance, you know, but she was always right with her mother. Mrs. Grove used to go to Amaranth—that was eight miles—to shop and one thing and another, and it was always after school with the horse and buggy. I know I went with her two or three times just to hold May on my knee and look after her while Mrs. Grove handled the horse.

Edward Elke: She was a mother to us. When it stormed real bad, when we couldn't get home, everybody got fed. Of course the school was supplied with a supply of plates and dishes and there was always food there, always emergency rations. She had lots of help, because everybody was willing to help Mrs. Grove. She was such a nice person.

Lydia Elke: When Mr. Grove taught school at Gladstone, he was gone a week, sometimes two weeks, and whenever it was stormy or, you know, lonesome there—well then my mother and dad they lived a mile north, they would let me stay overnight with her. Well to me this was about the greatest thing in the world, and so Mrs. Grove and I—I was not quite 14 but I was in grade 8, and was through as far as the school went at that time, you see, so we were very good friends, and I corresponded with her after she had moved away. Sometimes my brother Bill used to stay with her too if the weather was real bad.

Edward Elke: When he'd come from Gladstone, my brother Bill would put the lantern up on a big pole and then on a real clear night you could hear this little pony coming—or the team—for miles, and the frost and the cutter squeaking. This I remember quite well, on a real frosty day and not windy. And he had one of these big buffalo robes he used to wrap himself up in and one of those Santa Claus sleighs we used to call them. Well it was always night when he got home—it was frost right around this big buffalo robe right in there like snow.

Charlie Kuitner: (CHARLIE APPEARS AS THE YOUNG BROTHER IN *The Yoke of Life*, AND HIS OLDER BROTHER WAS A PROTOTYPE OF LEN) When he came to teach at Ferguson, he lived at Falmouth, his wife was there, but he drove to Ferguson with a team of horses and a cutter in the wintertime. He'd go back to Falmouth each night. We were two and a quarter mile from the school. And we walked that every morning and night, my brother and me. Kind of a mixed settlement. Some English returned men; not many Ukrainians, they were further north. It was German mostly. He could talk German. I think he was German, you know.

Lydia Elke: He was Austrian really, wasn't he?

Otto Baker: Quite a man. When I went to him, I was in grade 8. I learned more from old Grove than I did from all the others combined. But I tell you what he was most interested in, is in trees and plants. And—oh all kinds of animals. One thing—he wouldn't stand for swearing or anything like that. He just wouldn't stand for it. One guy he caught him swearing and he took him into the room and gave him a strapping. He didn't swear any more after that. He stripped him, you know. When he gave him a licking.

Rudolph Elke: He used to strap the odd boy at Falmouth; the older ones that Mrs. Grove couldn't handle—strap them for her. I remember this.

Roy Oswald: I remember there was an older boy, that was one of the Riedel boys, and I guess she wanted him to stay after four and he didn't. And next morning, Mr. Grove didn't drive to Ferguson. He was waiting for him. He took him into that extra little room there, the teacher's room, and son-of-a-gun, it was just like a war on for a while. Anyways he never came to school again after that.

Arthur Riedel: It was a dirty deal, the worst thing that any child ever had happen to him in school. He sent her to Ferguson that morning and he took our school. There was no justice in it. He wasn't even my own teacher and he had no authority in that school.

Lydia Elke: A lot of times she went to Ferguson school and he stayed and taught us here. That was after he hurt his knee. He had decided he was going to get three or four chickens, and he was making this chicken coop, and Mrs. Grove and I, we were sitting on the step outside, and he bangs a nail right into his knee. Oh he just wasn't a carpenter or anything like that whatsoever, but he tried everything. Anyway, that one winter he had a bum knee. They changed like that quite a lot of times that she went there and he stayed at Falmouth.

Elsie Elke: When she went to Ferguson, after she left the school she'd pass our place, the Elkes, a mile; then another mile, the Langners lived; and then another mile up there Kuitners lived, and the Lipkes and then another half-mile was the school. And there the Brandens lived just across the road from the school, you see. So every little —every mile there was someone.

Otto Baker: With our dad and mum, when he'd come to our place, he'd talk about the old country, mostly about travelling, and one thing I know my mother talked about—he was five years, say, in France and he was four years somewhere else, and he was a year here and a year there, and dad—again without letting on—he kept a mental count with that, and I think dad said that that man would have to be ninety years old. And you know—things like that. Well, I call it exaggeration.

Charlie Kuitner: They had a daughter May—they named the post office up at Ferguson there—they named the post office May Grove after the daughter. Brandens had it. They were Swedes. Oh I remember him. I liked him. But the life we used to lead was different from now. Two and a quarter mile, that's a nice little hike. I used to herd sheep in the morning, go to school, come back from school, hunt cows and milk them—I didn't milk cows in the morning because I had to herd sheep—and then I went to school and tried to learn. And if I didn't make out so good I got a licking to boot. My brother, he was older than I was and he went to the lumber camp, and after Grove left here he sent him books and wanted him to come back up to Rapid City or somewhere in there, you know, and go to school and go on higher up you see.

Otto Baker: The kids thought the world of him, you know. Tell you the truth, I think it was his stories. He made it so interesting. He could put emphasis on it—oh he'd bring it out something terrific you know. The kids were just waiting for that—it was as quiet as a mouse in school. Nobody would even breathe hardly. And yet we knew a lot of the time that everything was lies, but—

Lydia Elke: This was a new country, a challenge—something he used to talk about. He'd say, you know, what a challenge this was, and he enjoyed all the hardships that there were.

Otto Baker: Adventure, you know. Going to be a pioneer, more or less.

Roy Oswald: He was not writing here. But his memory was here, you see?

Grove began to use these memories almost immediately in the writing of *Over Prairie Trails,* as he used them in other books about the Big Grassy Marsh. He also used the name of Branden, the Swedish people who kept the May Grove post office, as the name of his hero in *A Search for America.*

But the romance of pioneering faded, and by the summer of 1919, having spent about two years in a homesteading area—which in later accounts he sometimes expanded to twenty—Grove emerged once more from German surroundings and went forward again with the Life Plan.

At the beginning of August, Mrs. Grove went to Winnipeg to take her normal school course and complete her second-class professional teacher's standing. Grove became a principal again, this time of the Consolidated Intermediate School at Eden, a village about the size of Haskett, where two thirds of the 95 pupils were brought to school by vans. Grove's salary was $1,500.

This time it was Mrs. Grove who made the wearying weekend trips home, and it was Grove who looked after house and child and taught during the week. Little May, now four, was taken to school by her father, where she sat quietly on a chair near her father's desk. In Eden as in Virden, a warmhearted woman came to his aid. Mrs. Gunn, though she had a two-year-old of her own and was expecting another baby, offered to have the little girl stay with her during school hours: "Mr. Grove rather twisted that in his book where he mentions my name as Mrs. Cannon and he said that on account of my little boy being lonely, his little girl played with him. But that was not quite the way it was. Little May used to come to my house and her father would come after school and—we lived above a hardware store—and he'd come into the hardware store and come to the foot of the stairs and call 'May!' and the little girl would get ready and go home with him." [11]

Grove makes clear his own attitude to May in *Over Prairie Trails* which he was then writing: "ever since the little girl was born, there had been only one desire which filled my life. Where I had failed, she was to succeed. Where I had squandered my energies and opportunities, she was to use them to some purpose. What I might have done but had not done, she was to do. She was to redeem me. I was her natural teacher. Teaching her became henceforth my life-work. . . . Deprived of her, I myself came to a definite and peremptory end. With her to continue my life, there was still some purpose in things, some justification for existence" (117–18). The characters here may be Rousseau and Emilie, but the notion is that of old John Elliot—that his children were to fulfill his own ambitions—and the parental attitude is the kind that drove Samuel Butler to write *The Way of All Flesh*.

Grove had been teaching at Eden less than three months when he sent in his resignation which the school board accepted on November 8, though he continued to teach until December 12, when his successor took over at a higher salary. It was beginning to be a pattern. Neither Mrs. Gunn nor Mrs. Albright, one of the women teachers, nor any of the former students of the area can recall any physical disability that prevented Grove from teaching, as he claims he had in *In Search of Myself*. Neither was there any recollection in the Falmouth area of a mishap other than the time when he drove a nail into his knee, which was well known and widely repeated. It seems much more likely that, just as with the dream of pioneering, so the high dream of "the sacredness, the responsibility of the teaching profession" had faded, and that Grove was being quite candid when he said in *Over Prairie Trails:* "We live for something—do not merely live. The wage-slave lives for the evening's liberty, the business man for his wealth, the preacher for his church. I used to live for my school" (118).

But another dream was taking its place. At the beginning of December he had sent his manuscript to McClelland & Stewart. With exemplary promptness they wrote him December 19, "We were able to give an early reading to your manuscript, 'Seven Drives Over the Manitoba Trails,'" and they proposed to publish it "next autumn."¹² His writing had been accepted; he was an author.

Mrs. Grove finished her normal school course; the family moved to Ashfield about twenty miles north of Winnipeg; and "Mrs. Tena Grove, Prof. II" signed the attendance record on January 4, 1920. Grove sent off a sample of "The Immigrant," the first title of *A Search for America*, and McClelland & Stewart wrote him on January 29: "We think you have a very important book in this, and shall be glad to receive later on any additional chapters"; he told them he was working on "Summer Showers," a companion volume to "Drives," and they were interested in that too. By the end of April he had completed a manuscript of "The Immigrant" and had sent it to them. At this point, Grove had one manuscript accepted for publication, another in the hands of the publishers, and still another under way. The early months of 1920 were buoyant with the feeling of having done the right thing to break away from teaching.

The buoyancy did not last long. The script of "The Immigrant" was returned; and, by the end of the summer, the publishers wrote: "We are sorry to have to disappoint you in connection with the publication of your book this year," but they had been unable to find an American publisher to support it. It was no doubt with a view to getting a recommendation from a respected authority that, in the fall of 1920, Grove wrote to the noted American naturalist, John Burroughs, whom he greatly admired, to ask if he might send Burroughs some of his "natural history" writing for his opinion. Burroughs evidently agreed, and so Grove sent what must have been the script of "Summer Showers," the first version of *The Turn of the Year*. Burroughs' reply would not have raised his spirits:

My dear sir,
I have received your roll of MS. which is much more than I bargained for. I expected to see only a sample of your natural history work. I find there is no natural history in this mass of matter. As literature, I am bound to tell you I do not think it has any special value and I doubt if an editor will take it. Bare, unrelieved description of storms or of any other phase of nature is tiresome. My own aim has been to interpret nature, not to describe her. One must be a philosopher as well as a naturalist to write well in this field.
I have not read all of your MS, but have dipped into it in many

places and find it all of a piece. I will return it to you when I receive the necessary stamps—60 cents in stamps.

Sincerely yours,
John Burroughs [13]

Altogether, it became depressingly clear that Grove's hope of gaining income from his writing had been premature, and so in May 1921, both of the Groves applied to Eden. In the interval, Eden had attained high school status, and it was in need of a high school principal as well as a teacher for the upper public school grades. The school board held an unusually short meeting on June 3: "Special Meeting called to consider applications for principal and teachers. Moved and seconded that we accept Mr. and Mrs. Grove's applications. Meeting adjourned." Salaries at Eden had gone up with the higher status. F. P. Grove got $1,920, and Mrs. Grove—the signature from now on is Catherine Grove—got $1,200. In view of Grove's constant plea for sympathy on grounds of penury, it is worth noting that their combined salary was not far short of that of the principal of Earl Grey Junior High School in Winnipeg, who got $3,300.[14]

In this time of uncertainty, Grove took steps to provide insurance against the future. In the summer of 1921 he applied for status as a naturalized Canadian, and he received his papers in December of that year. He had decided to stay. He was no longer an outlander. He also applied for permanent teaching certification, which he received on the special recommendation of Fletcher, the deputy minister. And he resumed his work for the bachelor of arts degree. Throughout the winter he took courses in eighteenth- and nineteenth-century French and German literature and in the modern German drama and novel. In the spring, as usual, he asked for and got special concessions, this time to allow him to write his examinations during his Easter vacation. Apart from French composition in which he got only 70 percent, he got A's in his courses, and at convocation on May 18, 1922, he received his degree. Coincidentally, the Gold Medal in French went to a Miss Johnston, who had been substituting at Eden from the beginning of May for a teacher who was ill.

But Grove's relations with students and school board had been increasingly uneasy. A former high school pupil, then fifteen years old and the son of a member of the school board, recalled a troubled year:

[54]

He never attained nor tried to attain any warmth of feeling with us. We respected him, admired his knowledge, writhed under his jibes, but never liked him.

In this regard—I was certainly not his favorite—I remember bearding my father one evening just before a school board meeting that was to terminate his stay. I begged my father to keep Mr. Grove, pleading his ability as a teacher. I don't know whether I had any influence, but he was kept on as principal for a further period. I cannot recall the reason for his dismissal. I have a feeling that it was on a personality basis between him and the school board.

I know that he had back trouble when he came back to Eden and wore a tightly laced support ("It takes two men to pull it tight enough" I think that was his remark.) The story was that he was involved in a car accident. He was thrown from a car 60 feet down a steep bank and landed on his feet. That was said to have torn some of his organs loose in the body cavity.

Mr. Grove was a complex character. But he was real. I guess I learned more under him than from any other teacher I had. Perhaps that is why I liked him in spite of himself.[15]

But before the "services no longer required" letter arrived, the Groves had applied to Rapid City, and on May 18 the *Rapid City Reporter* announced their appointments, Grove as high school principal, salary $2,200; Mrs. Grove as teacher of the senior public school grades, salary $1,200.

Of all the places in which the Groves lived, the little town of Rapid City, where they spent the next seven years, had the loveliest setting. A broad valley, well treed, with a river running through it and gently sloping hills rising around it, it was a place where a person might well think that here he could live and write. Within a few weeks of his becoming high school principal there, Grove's first book, *Over Prairie Trails*, was published.

PART II

The Writing Years, 1919-1929

The decade 1919–29 includes the writing of eight of Grove's twelve published books—from *Over Prairie Trails* to *Fruits of the Earth*—a number of unpublished works, most of the short stories, some verse, a few reviews, and several articles. It sees his quite remarkable rise within six years after his first publication in 1922 to become a dominant figure in Canadian letters.

Within the body of this writing are two groups of works that are loosely designed as trilogies. Very broadly they are divided by Rousseau's categories of the individual and the citizen. The first group, concerned partly with man and nature and more with the individual's self-realization, is the group set in the Big Grassy Marsh country, the Falmouth-Ferguson area. The three parts include the companion pieces of *Over Prairie Trails* and *The Turn of the Year*, *Settlers of the Marsh*, and *The Yoke of Life*. The second group is about man in society, the society of the family and of the world. It is the trilogy of generations that includes *Our Daily Bread* and two unpublished works, "The Weatherhead Fortunes" and "Jane Atkinson." Both groups show Grove working in large patterns but without successfully realizing them.

Following his determination to make a living as a professional writer, in the mid-1920's Grove tried a number of experiments: an attempt at the popular fiction of the detective story, a sortie into the esoteric world of James Branch Cabell who was creating a stir, a beginning in the age-old genre of the animal fable with the first version of what he called his "Ant Book." His experiments were as restless as his living had been; he tried as many new places in both, and he was tied to no particular region.

At the end of the decade there are two summing-up books: one, *It Needs to Be Said,* a collection of his papers and addresses on literary and other matters; the other, *Fruits of the Earth,* a re-vision or reconsideration of various elements of the two trilogies and so a kind of summation.

It is useful to consider this body of work in a roughly chronological order as to time of writing,[1] for the light that it sheds on Grove's thinking and on his explorations as a writer. It is convenient to begin with *A Search for America,* which is altogether outside of the Canadian scene. In addition, it is certainly one of the earliest works—Mrs. Grove said he had started on *A Search for America* before *Over Prairie Trails* was published,[2] and he did send his publisher a completed manuscript of it in May 1920. And finally it gives a broad basis thematically and structurally for a number of later works. As Branden says near the end of the book, "When I came from Europe I came as an individual; when I settled down in America, I was a social being."

CHAPTER 4

A Search for America[1]

A Search for America was by all odds the most popular of
Grove's works during his lifetime, and deservedly so, for it is
one of the best things he ever wrote. Yet it was seen by three
publishers before it was accepted in 1926 by a fourth. All professed to admire it, one calling it an important work, another
saying that he liked it and that it ought to be published; but all
looked askance at what one reader described as " a cartload of
manuscript." When The Graphic Publishers did accept it, they
insisted that it be cut, and Grove wrote to Watson Kirkconnell,
on November 25, 1926, that he had "ruthlessly" cut it to half its
original length. Half its original length ran to 448 pages in the
Graphic edition. The publishers' diffidence is understandable.

The elementary attraction of this historical novel, which Grove
set before the turn of the century, is the universal one of a good
story, with a great variety of scenes, experiences, and characters,
told with vigor. It has the attraction that the questing knight has
always had, and the form of this romance is as inevitable as
Chaucer's pilgrimage or Christian's journey: a beginning, many
episodes, and a happy ending. The picaresque nature of the story
of the road makes the addition or subtraction of episodes a matter
of the taste or the exigencies of the moment.

The more specific attraction, when the book came out in the
1920's, was the timeliness of its interwoven themes which caught
the attention of diverse people. Among the themes was the
plight of the immigrant, disillusion within the New World, the
disappearance of the hero figure, and the individual's transformation into adulthood—his finding of himself and of his life's work.
The shifts of title (Grove always had trouble with titles) show
that Grove himself was undecided about which aspect of the
book to emphasize; or they may indicate his deepening awareness
of the implications of it. In 1920 it is either "The Immigrant" or

"The Emigrant," each suggesting a different perspective; in 1923 he calls it "The Search for America," which has echoes going back at least to John Donne; but in 1927 he amends that to "A Search for America," which sharpens as it limits the application. Finally, he added a subtitle, "The Odyssey of an Immigrant," which calls up thoughts of another far traveler.

The story has two movements. In the mid-1890's, a young European dilettante, Phil Branden, aged twenty-four, who spends his time flitting about the Continent and in and out of universities, is jolted out of his pleasant life by his father's bankruptcy, which is quickly followed by ostracism from his fair-fortune friends. Rejected, he sails for the New World to seek his fortune, docks at Montreal, goes on to Toronto where he gets job as a waiter, leaves that to go to New York where he becomes a door-to-door book salesman, discovers that all the world is a cheat and so, penniless and disheartened, starts west as a tramp, following the path of the rivers, in quest of Abraham Lincoln and virtue.

After a time of near-starvation and some hallucinations, the young Diogenes finds his honest man in a country doctor and in a farm couple who nurse him back to health after a bout of pneumonia. That part of his quest has ended. He says to the doctor, "The Abraham Lincolns live all around. . . . You are one of them" (290). The hero figure had not disappeared; it had simply been transformed.

The second part of Branden's quest is to find his life's work, his niche. The doctor gets him a job in a small veneer factory while he recuperates, and, grown suddenly mature, he trains the other workers, sets the business on its feet, and then once more takes to the road, this time as a harvest-hand hobo, to find "the soil where I could grow." He follows the harvest up the Dakotas, gets a job on a huge farm of over twenty thousand acres, instructs its young owner in his moral obligations, going farther north finds a shyster cheating a Finnish immigrant of his land and labor, is chased out of the village by a venal policeman, gets work running a railroad handcar, crosses into Canada, and gets to Winnipeg with his harvest savings of $249.35. He had realized that his niche, his part of the world's work, was "to go to foreign settlements and help recent immigrants build their partial views of America into total views" (392). In the last half-dozen lines, young Branden gets a job as a teacher and starts on his life's work. In about two years after his arrival in Montreal, he has found America, he has found himself as "a social man"; he has found his place; the quest is successful, and the ending is happy.

The double movement of the quest motif is reflected in a variety of schematic contrasts: the two restaurants in Toronto; the two book companies in New York, one diddling little old ladies and one gulling millionaires; the two social areas of city and country; the two moral and geographic areas of the degenerate East and the virtuous West.

What could become a monotonous seesawing is averted, however, by an overriding pattern of ascending social values which determines the choice of episodes and their order. Book I, "Waiterdom," is the life of a menial, a form of slavery; Book II is the commercial world, the great con game, a corruption of human life and values; Book III ends with the veneer factory, which is desirable because it is the creativity of the industrial world, using human gifts, and is a proper outcome of education based on manual training and workshops; but of course Book IV comes, as it must, to the agricultural life, what Rousseau called "the earliest and most honorable of the arts," the root and crown of existence, from which all other forms take their being. Branden sees the vision of it as "the ground-mass of the nation—the soil from which cities sprang, like strange, weird, sometimes poisonous flowers in the woods. For the first time I saw the true relation: the city, the town working for the country: the farmer, though not yet realized as such, the real master of the world who would one day come into his own" (310).

Within the sections, the vigor of the narration overcomes any sense of a studied pattern. Individual episodes are carefully prepared, built to a peak, and gradually resolved. In the cheap restaurant, the waiters gather casually, exchange morning banter, and prepare their tables; a few customers enter, the tables begin to fill up, voices grow louder, the waiters' movements faster, the clash of dishes harsher until, behind the scenes in the kitchen,

a casual observer would have seen half-naked maniacs dancing and jumping about in crazy lunacy. In the corridor, waiters were bustling each other, reaching up into the dish-rack, flinging plates on the counter and bellowing orders at the top of their voices. From out of the reeking pit behind me came yelling shouts, repeating every order that was given. (52-53)

Gradually the fury of the noon hour rush subsides, and the waiters relax:

In surveying the room, I was struck as by the sight of a disaster. Every table-cloth was soiled; every shelf of the central racks and the dumb-waiters was piled with a jumble of dirty dishes. The atmosphere reeked with the smells of the kitchen. The battle was fought; we were left on the field. (54)

In the episode of riding the rods there is the additional quality of tension and danger—fear of being caught, fear of injury:

At last we were thundering along. The whole universe seemed to be one deafening bedlam of noise let loose. We swayed and swung as we were holding on for dear life, our hands getting sore from the pelting gravel, our eyes closed tight, our faces pressed down on our sleeves. The track seemed to be a succession of hills and valleys; the rods, a mere vibrating mass of whipping cords; our arms, springs now stretched to the snapping-point, now compressed beyond the power of re-expanding when the roadbed rose and pressed the steel-truck upward. I felt dazed and frightened beyond anything I had ever gone through. . . . (332)

But the action scenes are not the only effective ones. Grove often makes skillful use of silence, as he does in Branden's taking leave of the mute driftwood gatherer who had sheltered him:

Then I stopped and said, "I suppose, it's about time for me to be moving."
And something startling happened. The man spoke. He spoke with an effort, twisting his whole body in the act, the words sounding like those of an overgrown boy when he is changing his voice, hoarse, unexpectedly loud and husky. It looked and sounded as if he were heaving the words up from, let me say, his abdomen and ejecting them forcibly.
What he said was, "I reckon." (259)

Another notable passage is the vivid account of the world's dropouts, of hobodom:

It is characteristic of this unstable flood of floating labour that there is a great feeling of solidarity—when they are together in a crowd. Then they are the hobos, as opposed to the great, contemptible mass of the respectable citizens. . . . But when we met them singly or in smaller groups, that feeling of solidarity was non-existent. Every individual feels himself better than his neighbour; his neighbour is a "bum;" he himself is the Lord of Creation. . . .

Gradually there formed in my mind the impression of a vast exodus, or rather a vast confluence of numberless multitudes engaged in a pilgrimage to some Mecca (337).

The craftsmanship and the variety of such passages are admirable. The special knowledge of the cheap restaurant, of riding the rods, of the harvest hegira, and so on, give to this *roman vécu* that immediacy that places it in company, for instance, with Smollett's *Roderick Random*.

But it was not only the romance of the eccentric that attracted people to *A Search for America*. They also found in it familiar, popularly accepted myths, the Horatio Alger myth and the innocent immigrant myth.

It is entertaining to place Grove's story beside that of Kafka's *Amerika*, for when Kafka "conceived his novel in Prague in 1913," Klaus Mann wrote, "he knew no Americans at all and understood very little English." [2] Kafka's Karl, seduced at sixteen by a woman of thirty-five, is cast out by his family, breaks off his career in Europe, comes to America as to a rebirth, is cheated by swindlers, gets a job in a hotel, and is unjustly dismissed by a bullying head porter. The parallel between Karl and Grove's Branden indicates a recognized stock figure with stock experiences. But there is a further affinity between the two books that has to do with the style or manner of writing. When Klaus Mann speaks of Kafka's personal style as one "of dream-like romanticism and realistic exactness," he could also be describing the style of *A Search for America*, for while there is plenty of realistic exactness, there is also a remarkable degree of dreamlike romanticism in the book.

In the European beginning, for instance, cities are named, countries are named, desires are fulfilled, and senses are satisfied, but though the time is July and the father is six-foot-five and in his seventies, time, place, and people are actually vague. As in many a medieval romance, the light is on brilliantly colored figures who are featureless. Thus it is with the father who says to his son, "Don't let it for a moment enter your head that you should feel sorry for me. As I said, I am shaking off ill-fitting clothes in order to be better fitted. I see Paradise ahead" (8).

The New York interlude of Book II also has dreamlike qualities, though Branden calls it a nightmare. Again, hotels are named, and addresses are given; the Flatiron Building, the Public Library, and Fifth Avenue are all mentioned. When Branden calls on an official in "one of the most fashionable sky-scrapers of the city," he is taken to "the luxurious dining-room of a fashionable men's luncheon-club." This New York is not more intimate nor more vivid than the one that Kafka conceived in Prague.

As Kafka could dream up an America, as Coleridge could describe tropic seas and icebergs, neither of which he had seen, as Swift could create convincing worlds that never were, as Grove himself could recount, as he did later, a well-documented journey that he never took from Venezuela up through Nicaragua to the Colorado Mountains, so in *A Search for America* he used all his novelist's power in the imaginative forming of experience for his creature, Branden. But when the young novitiate starts west on his strange river journey in search of Abraham Lincoln, the dreamlike romanticism of the early part suffers a sea-change.

Having rid himself of his possessions, Branden starts west in the clothes he stands in, with a raincoat, a few toilet articles, and in his hip pockets two slim volumes, the New Testament and, of course, the *Odyssey*. On the level of actual behavior, Branden presents an astonishing sight as he purportedly seeks for the soul of America by creeping about, hiding behind bushes, shunning contact with men "for whom I still had nothing but aversion" (239), starving himself, suffering a fever fit, and finally coming down with pneumonia. It is a curiously puzzling course of action which seemingly does very little to advance the search.

But of course what the novel has entered upon is outright dream vision, and Grove makes that apparent in any number of hints and warnings. Apart from Branden's repeatedly saying that his search might not be a geographical search at all, the opening pages of Book III (225–28) are explicit as to the nature of what is to follow: "the chronology of events is confused. . . . The narrative must thus lose some of its connections; transitions will be missing; apparent contradictions will crop up; feelings, thoughts which are hard to reconcile. And there are, especially in the beginning, detached scenes, disconnected visions, like mere pic-

tures flashed upon the screen of memory, seemingly quite meaningless, and yet they belong into the tale of my tramps. The very
first memories are a series of mere visions." A little later, on his
first day on the road, "I feel strangely weightless. I am cut loose,
adrift on the world. . . . I seem to be weighing the time, as if
I held a certain mass of it in my hands." "Awakening is like a
resurrection." "I got used to being silent." "I was a wanderer in
the hills. Soon after I became a wanderer in the valleys."

What Branden finds in the hills and the valleys and the course
of the rivers is an interestingly literary world, the melding of old
and new, the legacy of European civilization, and its American
transmigration. An early encounter is with Ovid's *Metamorphoses,*
Baucis and Philemon somewhere in Pennsylvania but not yet
turned to trees; and there are some touches from Wordsworth's
"Michael." In case we should miss the point, Grove wrote, "oh,
how I wished I could leave a 'wonderful pitcher' behind!" Unfortunately, Grove's prose deteriorates under the pressure of the
highly sentimental scene; yet it is one which he was obviously
proud of, for he transferred it, using much of the same phrasing,
to the vignette of "Love in Autumn" in *The Turn of the Year,* and
it was at least an element in the creation of John Elliot of *Our
Daily Bread.*

The rivers as usual are the flowing waters of life, of time; they
are avenues of commerce: "Water is nothing inanimate. . . . Water
is company. . . . So long as I followed a river I was sure of sustain-
ing life" (237). And rivers are also the currents of literary tradition. It is on the Ohio that two more literary works enter the
dream vision of the outcast Branden. One is *Robinson Crusoe,*
that one book needful according to Rousseau, but it is hardly
surprising that in this geographical area Crusoe must jostle with
his much younger American counterpart. Huck Finn–Robinson
Crusoe–Branden shows great ingenuity in salvaging from the
river a kettle, a ham, a pumpkin, and then a kitchen table and
some logs with which he builds a raft and plies the river. It is
almost obligatory, under these circumstances, that he should
meet the driftwood gatherer whose face " closely resembled the
face of Mark Twain in Carroll Beckwith's portrait" (252). In his
search for America, Branden *becomes* Huck Finn, and he meets
Mark Twain on the river because "America" is to be found in

Mark Twain. It is a fine and wise stroke on Grove's part to make him silent.

But the literary vision is not over. The immigrant, too, is America, and on another "strange trip along the river" (323), this time on the Missouri somewhere between St. Louis and Kansas City, Branden meets the hobo Ivan who reminds him of both "Titian's paintings of the Lord of Christianity," and of Tolstoy's Sergei Ivanovitch—the latter a rather curious association, for Tolstoy's self-righteous philosopher was a cold fish—but he later turns into Levin the agriculturalist, the ideal human being, "the man who stands squarely upon the soil and who, from the soil, from his soil, reaches out with tentative mind into the great mysteries" (348–49). Grove was enamored of that sentence, and he used it repeatedly not only in novels but also in the address that he gave from coast to coast on Nationhood. The culmination of the literary encounters is in the great gathering of the hobos, the lords of creation, "each of them a coarser and de-sublimated Henry David Thoreau" (322).

But the search for America is not only a search for the spirit of a country; it is a search for, the discovery of, "I, myself." It is to this theme of the soul's purging and its renewal that chapter headings—"The Descent," "The Depths," "The Level"—as well as various references to the inferno and to purgatory inescapably direct us. The long middle section of isolation is the trial, the testing of the novice, the metamorphosis from adolescence to adulthood, the rebirth of the individual. It is Rousseau's thesis at the beginning of Book IV in *Emile*, "We are born, so to speak, twice over; born into existence, and born into life; born a human being, and born a man." This twofold aspect of the book's structure is a characteristic one with Grove, repeated in various ways in later novels, and in this one of course a counterpart to the twofold movement of the quest.

The imagery of birth and transformation is diffused, implied in the coming to the New World as entering a new element, in the huge, womblike halls of the pier at Montreal and at Penn Station, in the chapter heading, "I Submerge," and in the strange water passage that Branden takes. It makes understandable the curious isolation from men as wet, cold, shrunken, Branden makes his way to the country of Abraham Lincoln. On the level of realism, of the actual story, this is incoherent, senseless; on the level of imagery it is the fetus making its way to birth. The birth, the leaving of the river, the time of fitful consciousness—the bout of pneumonia—the difficulty of emerging into human life, is quite fittingly attended by a doctor and a midwife.

Another image in the theme of self-discovery and associated both with the river and with metamorphosis is that of the frog. As a waiter, having "arrived at an undervaluation of myself," Branden says, "I lived, as it were, on the sea-level; I had the perspective of the frog: above him all things loom" (72). The same self-abasing image—"I had to restrict my view of it [America] to the view from below, to the perspective of the frog"— precedes Branden's decision to become a hobo, independent and proud. The frog, of course, is amphibious, if humble; it is adaptable. Then too, in its life course it is a dramatic example of metamorphosis, and so it serves to sharpen the implication of Branden's metamorphosis.

Also related to the theme of self-discovery is the clothing image. As Rousseau insisted, the essential man, the "I, myself," existed independent of the social order or of vocation. They are only outer clothing. This image begins in the first few pages with the father, a peasant's son who had married a wealthy woman now dead, and who, having lived all the fifty years of his married life in "ill-fitting clothes," proposes to cast them off, after "a lifetime of disguise" (9). The image continues in the elaborate and unsuitable wardrobe that young Branden brings with him to the New World, particularly the "stack of overcoats," which are peeled off one by one as he loses his European dream and sells the clothing, "suit after suit, overcoat after overcoat" (143). As with the fetus image, this image is ludicrous on the level of literal fact.

Closely connected with clothing and with the idea of transformation, of metamorphosis, is the motif of masks and masquerades. Faces, of course, are masks, and Branden had been trained "never to betray an emotion, to keep his mask intact," not to allow anything to alter "the impenetrable mask of my face." It is a strange reversal for him, an ironic masquerade, when he sees his face looking out of a newspaper at him and labeled "Clever crook" (129). The masquerade permeates the New York experience, from the two con men who fleece Branden of his money to the book racket, "a con-game on a gigantic scale," of which he becomes a part. Branden's job as a waiter, too, though an honest one, was still to him "bearable only when viewed as a lark, as something which you might do in disguise or for a very short time" (97).

Names also are a part of the masquerade. Hannon and Howard sound much more respectable than their aliases "Han the Hook" and "Big Heinie," but not only criminals hide behind other names. At the beginning of the book there is "The Hon." who had returned from South Africa after making his fortune as a hotel keeper under an assumed name. At the end of the book, the Tolstoy figure says, "Call me Ivan." But the most protracted example of pseudonymous living is that of Branden's short-term Toronto friend, Frank the waiter, who turns out to have a remarkable flair for circumstantial lies in the false New York references and addresses that he gives Branden. At one point, the two discuss the subject of assumed names.

"Carroll's as little my real name as yours is Branden."
"Just a moment," I interrupted him. "Is there no law in this country against assuming a false name?"
"No," he said. "There isn't. Not so long as you do it without dishonest purpose. Of course, if you do it for fraud—"
"Good," I interrupted him once more. "That settles that point. I don't see anything wrong in a man's changing his name if he cares to do so, law or no law. But since you've done it, I'm glad it isn't illegal" (80-81).

In the course of his search, Branden concludes that it is not family—a man's name—that is important; nor geography—where he goes; nor vocation—what he does. The important thing is what he is: "Here I stood entirely on my own feet. Whatever I might have to go through, if finally I arrived somewhere, if I achieved something, no matter how little, it would be my own achievement; I must be I" (30). And in that resolution is the metamorphosis from adolescent to adult, to the man who, coming upon the Finnish immigrant being swindled "put down the incident for what it was: an incident. It no longer clouded my whole horizon for me." (391)

It is the passage from the world of Innocence to the world of Experience, it is the myth of the innocent immigrant, with the paradoxical turn that old Europe is the world of innocence and new America the world of experience. The paradox exhibits the essential theme of the book: the search is indeed not geographical but universal. We are all immigrants in a strange world.

The sense of perspective that Branden has discovered in himself, however, leads him to make other distinctions. The fundamental difference between this country and Europe is that "The whole civilisation of Europe is based on the theory of the original sin. . . . But here there is a profound suspicion that in his heart the human animal wants to do right and is good" (378). And he senses "the great undercurrent of an evolution towards fairness, towards that which is morally right and true" (322). This evolution is accompanied by "a fact of literary history: John Burroughs was coming into his own. . . . It was the movement away from the accidentals of life and towards the essentials." (218) In other words, the Romantic movement is triumphant, that movement which Burroughs carried on in the United States from his literary progenitor Thoreau, who in turn perpetuated the European movement of Rousseau, Wordsworth, Froebel and others.

Yet the theme of the lost America undoubtedly added to the popularity of Grove's novel. The Age of Reform in the United States, goaded by the muckrakers, had given place to the Age of Disillusion by the time of Grove's revisions in 1926. Sinclair Lewis had already published chastisements of the middle class; Dos Passos was at work on his panoramic denunciation; and the Lost Generation were trying to see what they could do in a world they did not make—nor like. *A Search for America,* while it was fundamentally at variance with them, nevertheless seemed to be in accord with the widespread *mea culpa* mood.

CHAPTER 5

The Books of the Big Grassy Marsh[1]

A T THE time Grove was assembling the history of two years in the life of Phil Branden, he was also shaping the immediate experience of the two years in his own life which, in the fall of 1919, he was just concluding. At the end of *A Search for America,* middle-aged narrator-Branden says that he became a teacher and worked for over twenty years in immigrant communities. The two years from July 1917 to July 1919 include the one period when middle-aged author Grove actually did teach and live among recent immigrants, though when the Groves arrived to make their home in the Big Grassy Marsh country, a daily train service ran through Glenella, fifteen miles west, a tri-weekly service was on the branch line to Amaranth seven miles east, and there were enough settlers and settling to warrant the two schools of Ferguson and Falmouth, four and a half miles apart. This was as close as Grove ever got to "the wilderness," and he did not stay long.

He shaped that experience into two kinds of writing, a series of nature sketches and two novels, published as four books: *Over Prairie Trails,* 1922; *The Turn of the Year,* 1923; *Settlers of the Marsh,* 1925; and *The Yoke of Life,* 1930. If the publication covered eight years, the writing of the books seems to have covered six, from the completion of *Over Prairie Trails* in 1919, to Grove's sending A. L. Phelps the manuscript of *The Yoke of Life* in the summer of 1925, at that stage under the title of "Equal Opportunities." [2] The novels, together with the two series of sketches which form really one book, make a loose trilogy in which Grove probed the individual in his relation to nature and in his relation to other people.

In the probing, Grove was applying concepts from the Rousseau-Thoreau-Burroughs body of theory. The similarity in the elements of the names of that trio so pleased Grove's fancy that he coined the name THOROUGH in a footnote that appears in the first, unpublished, version of the "Ant Book." It is quite possible that the name Thurow Castle, which he claimed as his native home in *In Search of Myself,* had the same origin, and that the home was his spiritual home.

I Over Prairie Trails and *The Turn of the Year*

For the sketches, Grove followed Burroughs, whom he often quotes, more devotedly than Thoreau, for Burroughs was the more precise, exacting, detailed of the two in the descriptions of what he saw and heard. This kind of writing particularly appealed to Grove with his special interests in mathematics and nature study, and so there is the meticulous detail ("He made the first mile in seven and a half minutes . . . then came the turn to the west . . . and I had to follow it for half a mile") together with the wonder of the natural world; or as Grove says, "This is only one-quarter a poem woven of impressions; the other three-quarters are reality" (41). Unfortunately, his cataloguing of observed details became so exhaustive and relentless in *The Turn of the Year* as to call forth the cry of pain from Burroughs. Certainly, nothing could be more flatly factual than the titles that he first gave to these two complementary volumes of sketches: "Seven Drives Over Manitoba Trails," and "Summer Showers on the Plains." The publishers rescued them from that handicap.

The seven sketches in *Over Prairie Trails* recount seven trips that Grove took on weekends from Gladstone to Falmouth during the 1917–18 winter.

In the opening essays the style is like that of the horse, "swinging along, though in a leisurely way, yet without hesitation." It is a world of leisure. There is time to look about. There is immense space. Throughout the land, there are scattered houses, there are clumps of trees, there is a shy wolf, a rabbit, a partridge; and there is the little group of the man, the buggy, and the horses with their comfortable clop-clopping along the road, a world-within-world. It is a quiet land, in which the man feels "the absolute friendliness of all creation for myself" (13).

The tone of the writing is pleasantly attractive; the narrator is unassuming, likable, believable. He has a sense of humor and so has his horse: "When we met a team and pulled out on the side of the road, he would take it for granted that I desired to make conversation. He stopped instantly, drew one hindleg up, stood on three legs, and drooped his head as if he had come from the ends of the world" (3). The prose is lively but not strained, and it has an agreeable variety in its rhythms as for instance in the lines on the goldfinches when, after three phrases of similar pattern, the next phrase takes a fine sweep out in the larger cadence of the bird's movement, and then comes to rest as it ought to do: "All over this vast expanse, which many would have called a waste, there were strings of them, chasing each other in their wavy flight, twittering on the downward stretch, darting in among the bushes, turning with incredible swiftness and sureness of wing the shortest of curves about a branch, and undulating away again to where they came from" (6). Here is writing that is controlled, poised, skillful, and convincing: this is the way it was at that time in that place, and we feel grateful that someone took the pains to put down these things and so preserve them.

In the succeeding essays the traveler goes by night, by day, in storm, along different routes. He sees the glory of hoarfrost, the terror of snow, the majesty of a grove of tall poplars, and in the skeleton of a stable he sees that "The wilderness uses human material up." Fog and mist blot out the land and constrict the world so that his two lamps make "a very small room, this space of light—the buggy itself, in darkness, forming an alcove to it" (32). Nature becomes stern rather than beneficent as wind and snow take over: "Altogether there was an impression of barren, wild, bitter-cold windiness about the aspect that did not fail to awe my mind; it looked inhospitable, merciless and cruelly playful" (66). On the last journey, menace comes from above, from the sky: "Hardly ever had I seen . . . a sky that with its blackness and its massed multitudes of clouds looked so threatening, so sinister, so much like a battle-array" (142). Three mishaps on this trip, when for the first time he did not reach the end, his home, put fear in both man and horses: "To this very hour, I am convinced that the skies broke my nerve that night" (145).

So the narrative goes—a chapter from Wordsworth's *Prelude,* in which the awe and power of nature once more assert their shaping force over the life of man. This overall narrative theme has its inner motions of suspense and victory in each of the drives when the man achieves his home, the warm human world, the young wife and their two-year-old daughter, the lantern gleaming in the winter night.

But the firm prose of the beginning of *Over Prairie Trails* wavers in the later episodes. Affectation creeps in with elegant inversions: "Slowly, slowly came the dawn" (49), "like an epic stretch my memories" (50), "Anxiety there was hardly any now" (127); with tasteless posing, "We spurned the miles, and I saw them not" (51); with frequent exclamation marks; and with strained images such as that of clouds hanging on "an enormous system of parallel clothes-lines . . . and like huge, black udders the outfolds were hanging down" (135-36). By these various attempts at heightened importance, Grove destroyed the forthright, flexible prose that makes the opening sections so admirable.

As the prose weakens, so does the quality of the narrator. Self-confidence gives way to self-pity as Grove creates for himself a character plagued by "incurable" illness, age, and poverty. The low point comes when he gives his reason for writing the book: "Surely, surely, I owe it to them, staunch, faithful hearts that they were, to set down this record so it may gladden the lonesome twilight hours that are sure to come . . ." (58). The ellipsis is his.

The nostalgic, long, long ago note in those lines is an example of one way in which Grove altered time to create his fictional fact. Characteristically, he expanded time to give an effect of long experience, of depth of knowledge, of judgment based on perspective. Such is the effect when he says that he took these trips some years ago, or when he speaks of an aspect of granite: "In front of my wife's cottage up north there lay an exfoliated rock in which I watched the process *for a number of years*" (my italics).

The free altering of fact to create fiction in *Over Prairie Trails* undoubtedly resulted for Grove in a truer account for himself; that is, it presented his emotional truth. In these sketches he is at great pains to call forth sentimental reactions as he portrays himself as righteous, just, kind, brave—and martyred. His deliberate creating of this actor is related to "the feeling of estrangement, as it were—as if I were not myself, but looking on from the outside at the adventure of somebody who yet was I" (86). This is the theme of the essence of the individual which he explored in the other books of this group, which is in young Branden's "I must be I," in Grove's unceasing search for himself, and in Thoreau's reflection in "Solitude":

> I know only myself as a human entity; the scene, so to speak, of thoughts and affections; and am sensible of a certain doubleness by which I can stand as remote from myself as from another . . . a part of me which, as it were, is not a part of me, but a spectator. . . . When the play, it may be a tragedy, of life is over, the spectator goes his way. It was a kind of fiction, a work of the imagination only, as far as he was concerned.[3]

This theme, which was of such vital importance to Grove, incidentally brings up a query as to who wrote Grove's books. In *Over Prairie Trails*, was it the aging, sick, poor man who struggled each week to Falmouth? Was it the stern, sardonic school principal of forty who was writing about it in Eden? Was it yet a third person who called himself Grove? Or was it Andrew Rutherford, the name that he proposed to the publishers as a pseudonym for the author? The highly uncandid Author's Preface only adds to this Chinese box. Perhaps Grove considered himself a fiction.

If the publishers were responsible for delaying the appearance of *Over Prairie Trails* until 1922, Grove was responsible for delaying *The Turn of the Year* until 1923. After he first mentioned it to McClelland & Stewart in January 1920, the publishers repeatedly inquired about it, but they did not receive the manuscript until January 1923, three years later. Possibly Burroughs' reaction had something to do with Grove's hesitation; at any rate, McClelland & Stewart also read it with dismay. There were two main problems: it was dull and it was much too short—surely the only time that a publisher had cause to complain about the latter in Grove. The publishers returned the manuscript with suggestions for getting "suspense and dramatic interest in it," for rounding it out to "about half as much more material as you have submitted" so that it would be about the same length as *Over Prairie Trails*, and of possibly taking a lead from a recent English book, *Colin Clout's Calendar*, to work out a cycle of the seasons.

The nucleus of *The Turn of the Year* is again weekend trips that Grove took to Falmouth, this time to and from the Leifur school (he called it Hnafur) near the shore of Lake Manitoba. There is a hobo meeting of crows; mosquitoes so thick they cast a shadow; glittering butterflies; the song of the meadowlark; catalogues of trees, flowers, and herbs, especially "the great willow-herb—Epilobium angustifolium—of Thoreau fame"; analysis of rain, cloud formations, air currents, and of soil composition. There is no doubt about the conscientious recording of details, but it is the record of the pedant, the private textbook for classes in nature study and in elementary physics. As Burroughs said, "Bare, unrelieved description of storms or of any other phase of nature is tiresome."

The writing is also pretentious. Clumps of words are designed to show the author's learning: "the more complex organisms of the Umbelliferae, Leguminosae, and Compositae appear" (82). A Latin quotation interjected in remarks about a sprinkle of rain—"parturiunt montes; nascetur ridiculus mus"—is simply funny, suggesting a brand of Latin coming from the foreign words and phrases at the back of the dictionary. There is rhetorical pretension: "How could I forget you, oh thickets and tanglewood copses, so long?" (79). There is more strained imagery. In the storm, the wind is a wild cat, a snarling dog, raindrops are a host of enraged marmoset monkeys. And then the depth of the bathetic is reached. "That master above who was coming to set the world to order again steps right over me and standing astride above me, seems to stop for an impalpable second before he empties out the bag of his wrath. And then he does it" (108).

Grove's limitations in the Thoreau-Burroughs type of nature essay are abundantly clear in this second volume. It was not enough to have a background in mathematics and nature study, nor was it enough to be deeply in sympathy with the naturalists. And Grove realized it. These two little books are one of the many experiments in writing that he tried, but just as he later abandoned others, he never again attempted nature studies in book form. He was not to become the Canadian "Thorough."

Yet *The Turn of the Year* has another kind of interest that comes from the material that Grove used to try to stretch his manuscript out to book length, as his publishers urged him to. His catalogues and his seasonal realism have a long heritage, and it may be Colin Clout who was responsible for the woodcut figures who move stiff-jointed through his pages. Two such figures appear in separate sketches as the Sower and the Reaper, or the Harvester. The Sower is an apelike old man, an Icelander, once a sailor, whose wife and children have left him: "Their place was taken by a strange idea in his mind: he was working for God, not for Man. Seeding and reaping became an obsession with him; or, better, perhaps, a religious exercise." This symbolic figure of the biblical sower appears also as Sigurdsen in *Settlers of the Marsh* and as one aspect of the patriarch John Elliot in *Our Daily Bread*. The silent, Slavic Harvester is another apparition of the Tolstoyan Ivan from *A Search for America*, with two passages repeated word for word. He is the saint-farmer and the natural man in organic unity with the soil.

It was not only Spenser, the Bible, and Tolstoy that contributed to *The Turn of the Year*. Ovid's *Metamorphoses* crops up again too. Baucis and Philemon, as love grown old, have moved from Pennsylvania, but the journey has not improved them. If they were sentimental outside Pittsburgh, they are maudlin in Manitoba. They provide one of the three "Vignettes"—love in spring, love in summer, love in autumn—with which Grove tried to fulfill the publisher's plea for dramatic interest. The two characters are called John and Ellen, and very shortly they appear in *Settlers* as the good lovers, Niels and Ellen. The vignette of "Love in Spring" presents them as two children of the soil, the plowing boy and the harrowing girl, children of nature, who are, of course, chaste. In fact, in *The Turn of the Year* all nature is virginal, pristine, chaste, a vast immaculate conception. Such a view of nature comes no doubt from Rousseau's "Everything is good as it comes from the hands of the Author of Nature," as well as from a conception of "the wilderness" as at least symbolically a representation of the days of creation.

Another symbol that appears in *The Turn of the Year* is further developed in *The Yoke of Life*, the symbol of the Lake. The significance that Grove attached to it is made clear in a brief passage from the first version of *The Yoke of Life*: "the wilderness had exerted its influence: what is wilder, what more intensely and irreducibly wild than the sea? And the Lake is a favourite daughter of the sea" (the fourth scribbler, p. 31). The storm on the lake in *The Turn of the Year* is one of death and destruction, the death of the year, the death of man, "the myriads of fish that were caught in the surf . . . lay dead, bared to the sun and awaiting the scavengers of the wild" (222). It is the forerunner of the storm when Len and Lydia, lashed together, carry out their suicide pact. But in both scenes of death, there is a promise of resurrection: "Life is dying: lie low till it re-awakes!"

The interlocking of the books which Grove set in the Big Grassy Marsh is more obvious in *The Turn of the Year* than in *Over Prairie Trails*, but it is there also, not only in the I-not-I theme, but in a lesser way in the repeated emphasis on the white range-line house with its majestic poplar bluff: "There hangs a story by this house. Maybe I shall one day tell it . . ." (11). It is the story of *Settlers of the Marsh*.

II *Settlers of the Marsh*

Grove's original plan for this work was a panoramic one that he called a "Three Book Series entitled LATTER-DAY PIONEERS." A pencil-written version sets the series out as

I The Settlement
II The White Range-Line House
III Male and Female.

After this outline comes a list of characters in four groups according to their nationality: five English, five Scandinavian, five German (but one is crossed out), and five Slav.

These characters appear, even if only in glimpses, in the first typed version of Book I, entitled "Settlers of the Marsh," consisting of 203 single-spaced pages. Book II of this version is 185 single-spaced pages entitled "The White Range-Line House; A Story of Marsh and Bush." The only version of Book III known to exist is in five hand-written examination booklets, but apparently it did exist in much longer form. In this trilogy, Book I, "Settlers of the Marsh," ends with Niels Lindstedt's disastrous marriage, the shock that it gave the settlement, and Ellen's reproachful "Niels, how could you!" Book II, "The White Range-Line House," covers the five years of Niels's married misery, his killing of his wife, and his leaving to give himself up, murmuring "Hanged by the neck until dead." Book III covered the next seven years, of Niels's trial, imprisonment, release, return, and final reconciliation with his true mate, Ellen.

According to letters that passed between Grove and Professor A. L. Phelps, Book I was complete by the early summer of 1923, Book II by September, and Book III by some time in 1924, since in December Phelps advised Grove to compress the account of the jail and the return to Ellen, because it was too detailed and tedious. In the meantime, in January 1924, Grove had sent Book I to McClelland & Stewart who, faced with a dismal failure in *The Turn of the Year,* turned it down, saying that it would be too risky, that it would not sell widely. He then sent it to Macmillan (it must have been by the next mail) who also rejected it but who gave him the benefit of the criticisms they had received from three readers: "The book, as far as we can judge, adheres closely to truth in its depicting of the life of the pioneer in the un- cleared bush country. Your painting of . . . the ignorance, brutality and crime which it engenders is an absolutely truthful one. But we think the tale is far too long. In 203 pages of closely written manuscript you set forth a story which we suggest might have been much more effectively presented in two thirds of the space. . . . It seems to us that condensation is greatly to be desired and yet we feel that with your avowed purpose of a trilogy in mind, such a suggestion perhaps would not be particularly welcome to you" (February 25, 1924).

Gradually, as a result of rejections from publishers and admoni- tions from Phelps—including, "I don't think you can get the wor. 'bugger' published in Canada"—Grove compressed the trilogy into one manuscript of eighty thousand words which, under Phelps's guidance, he sent at the beginning of April 1925 to Lorne Pierce of the Ryerson Press. Pierce accepted it and brought it out the following September under the title of *Settlers of the Marsh.* It is, in effect, Book II, with parts of Book I as introduction, and the five examination booklets of Book III as the ending.

This chronicle covers about eighteen years in the life of Niels Lindstedt who, around the turn of the century, comes out from Sweden as a young man and takes up a homestead in the newly opened area on the edge of the Big Grassy Marsh. He prospers, falls in love with Ellen Amundsen, and builds a home in anticipa- tion of marriage, but he is rejected by Ellen who, because of her father's brutishness to her mother (both now dead), has vowed that she will not marry. Niels, a virgin himself, is seduced by Clara Vogel, a widow six years older than he and full of guile. Niels marries her, ignorant of the fact that she is the district whore. Over a period of five years, their marriage goes from bad to worse. Niels is finally told of her past; he finds her entertaining two men in their house; and he shoots her. He serves six and a half years of his ten-year sentence for manslaughter, returns to his farm, is reconciled with Ellen, and at the age of forty begins life anew.

The overall pattern is clear and familiar enough: It is the same as that of *A Search for America*: rejection, degeneration, a crisis, purging, regeneration. It is the individual in search of himself, tested by strange circumstances. As Niels thinks to himself, "Are there in us unsounded depths of which we do not know ourselves? Can things outside of us sway us in such a way as to change our very nature? Are we we? Or are we products of circumstance?" (166).

Both Branden and Lindstedt, as immigrants, are unusually innocent, both in their early twenties, as they enter into the unknown world of experience. Both have a Byronic aloofness, "alone, even in a crowd." But both men are physically isolated for a time, Branden because he deliberately evades human companionship, Lindstedt because no one in the district will come to the whore's house. Where Branden passes through the crisis of physical illness, Lindstedt's is a mental one, from which he recovers in prison. The kind country doctor who nurses Branden back to health is transformed into a kind prison warden who encourages Lindstedt to take evening classes and pass his high school examinations in mathematics and science. The state prison is a paradoxical freedom from the imprisonment of his life during his marriage. Both Branden and Lindstedt come to a happy, if muted ending. They have passed through experience to regeneration, to a purpose in life. Essentially, neither story has anything to do with pioneer life nor with the immigrant.

But the purgation of Niels Lindstedt is not just the rebirth of the soul, the movement of *A Search for America;* it has another dimension, or it belongs to another genre. It is a saint's life. Professor Phelps, an ordained Methodist minister, sensed this fact when he suggested "The Passion of Niels" as an alternative title for the book, and perhaps it is not surprising that it was the Ryerson Press, the publishing house of the Methodist church, that accepted it. This publisher too, no doubt, recognized it for what it was.

The signposts are plain enough. Setting out to conquer the wilderness, Niels finds there Mrs. Vogel who "looked very lovely, he thought; but she looked like sin" (54); later on, "she looked like a relic of ancient temptation" (91). She tempted him and he did eat; his carnal nature betrayed him and he fell. For that Fall, "The Wages of Sin is Death!" (138). As the torment grows within him, "he could be seen driving furiously and aimlessly over the Marsh, his hair growing longer and longer on his shoulders, his beard flowing over his breast. . . . The story went that Lindstedt was insane; that he was a hermit, that he kept his wife a prisoner on his place. . . . Nobody would have come to the road to exchange a greeting with Lindstedt" (167). "He felt old, tremendously old, centuries old" (172); he reads and rereads Ecclesiastes. Finally there is the sacrificial blood-letting, the ritual killing. "That too," the warden tells him, "was in the atonement." (201).

In one of the earlier versions of the novel, Grove gave a clear directive. After the marriage, Clara, who used to work in the book department of a city store, begins to read a great deal. One of the books is Flaubert's *Temptation of St. Anthony* (in translation, of course). Although the reference is omitted in the published version, the scene of Clara's denunciation of Niels and her threat of revenge, one of the most powerful scenes in the book, follows very closely certain passages in Flaubert. Hilarion denounces St. Anthony: "Your chastity is but a more subtle kind of corruption and your contempt for the world is but the impotence of your hatred against it! . . . you have no pity save for your own wretchedness. You are so much swayed by a kind of remorse, and by a ferocious insanity, that you would repel the caress of a dog or the smile of a child." And the Queen of Sheba curses him: "You will repent. You will groan; you will be sick of life! But I will mock at you!" [4] Clara accuses Niels, "You prove to me that you are mean, brutal, revengeful. . . . This house . . . is going to be a famous house on the Marsh; its name is going to be a by-word ringing through the countryside, and you are going to be the laughing-stock of the settlement. Mark my words, you will rue this day!" (158).

With the two women Ellen and Clara, the symbolism is far from subtle. They are day and night, soul and body, the virgin and Eve, good and evil, country and city, virtue and sin, sacred and profane love: "One was a mate; the other, a toy" (57). As for Ellen and Niels, they are the two figures of "Love in Spring" from *The Turn of the Year,* children of the land and therefore innately virtuous.

Yet there is a curious sterility, a denial of life among all three protagonists. With Clara, the whore—"Death-in-life" as Niels calls her—this barrenness is a stock connotation; the source of life is defiled. But Ellen also renounces fruitful union. Death in life is her legacy from the past, from her parents. It comes from her father's lust, his brutish subjection of her mother, and the resultant miscarriages that her mother brought on that wasted her life. Dying, the mother implored, "Ellen, whatever you do, never let a man come near you." And Ellen solemnly swore "to God and to you" that she would not. Thereby she denies fruitfulness to herself and to Niels. Niels, however, has his own kind of barrenness. Like Ivan of *A Search for America*, he came to the New World with a dream "of himself and a woman, sitting of a midwinter night by the light of a lamp and in front of a fire, with the pitter-patter of children's feet sounding down from above" (36), but the wife had been a symbol merely; women to him were "vague schematic figures." The only one who had reality for him was his old peasant mother who scrubbed floors for the local baron and gathered sticks in his park for fuel. Her memory dominates his life. At first he identifies Ellen with her; later his old neighbor, Sigurdsen, the Sower of *The Turn of the Year*, seems to fuse with the image of his mother, giving the first appearance of the hermaphroditic creator that recurs in Grove's other novels. Niels comes, however, to love Ellen as his true mate, and when she rejects him, he decides that "woman would have no place in his life." He sees himself as a member of a nonreproducing race, "a race doomed to everlasting extinction and yet recruited out of the wastage of all other nations" (119), an idea that serves to establish a symbolic identity between Niels and his Percheron gelding, Jock. When, after shooting Clara, Niels goes to the stable and kills Jock, it is a symbolic suicide, for of course the death-in-life part of Niels must be destroyed before there can be a resurrection, an awakening of the soul.

The sterility is closely linked with the theme of slavery, real or apparent, which is a constantly recurring theme with Grove. There is the man Dahlbeck, a slave to lust, which was "the defiling of an instinct of nature: it was sin"; and Niels sees himself "bond-slave to a moment in his life, to a moment in the past, for all future times" (138). As he is a slave in his marriage, so is the woman, and when he refuses to release Clara, she justly accuses him: "You don't want me any longer. But I am not to belong to any one else. I am to be your property, your slave-property." Niels, the man who had left the Old World because of the brutalizing of women, who had vowed that his wife would not be a slave, is now no better than Ellen's father, who subjected his wife by brute force.

There is also slavery to the land. This, too, is a distortion of the ideal that Niels first had: "Land I've cleared is more my own than land I've bought," as his friend Nelson said. But as Niels prospers—"the farm owned him; not he the farm. . . . It grew according to laws of its own" (116).

Out of the land and the prosperity had arisen the house, "the mansion," the dream of the small peasant boy shivering as he waited for his mother outside the Baron's home. The white rangeline house is the symbol of Niels's success; it is the house of his dream. The symbol of the house recurs many times in Grove's work, "the mansion"—here so oddly applied to two stories of four rooms and a lean-to—but whenever the symbol occurs, it is a mockery of the dreams and hopes of him who built it. Here it becomes the shell for a life of hell on earth. But it is regenerated. This "mansion" is another symbol that follows the course of Niels's life: the ideal, chaste and empty; the invasion, its decoration for a life of luxury and evil, the debasing of sex within it till it becomes the whore's house; the destroying of the evil within it, its cleansing and refurbishing by Ellen, Niels's return to it after his atonement. The house will fulfill the dream: "What will unite them is love" (216).

The cycle of the life of Niels and of the house is the world within world, the microcosm-macrocosm concept that fascinated Grove. In the widest connotation it is once more the nature myth, the death and rebirth of the year and of the god—the novel begins in November and ends with the renewal of spring—and in the background behind the main figures is the procession of the seasons with the plowing, sowing, blossoming, reaping, sleeping, reawakening, the eternal death and resurrection which is the fundamental movement of comedy. With Virtue not only triumphant but rewarded, Grove underlines the elemental nature of Niels and Ellen by having them, now in middle age, repeat the ritual mating dance of twelve years before. Then it was autumn, a storm came. Now the sky is fair and it is spring. "They sit and look out, as if in a resurrection of what was dead" (216). There had to be a happy ending. It is essential to the meaning of the book which is a cosmic comedy.

Apart from the calendar of activities, there is little left in *Settlers of the Marsh* of the pulsating life of the community that gave meaning to the title as Grove first used it. What there is of it is connected with the Lunds, particularly Mrs. Lund and their adopted son, Bobby. Mrs. Lund comes to be the substitute mother for Niels, and Bobby his substitute son, who works on Niels's farm. Bobby is the sole figure in the most masterful scene of the book: the silent farmyard on the night when Niels kills Clara.

But in spite of the care that obviously went to its devising and in spite of moments of excellence, *Settlers of the Marsh* is a disappointing book. The prose is often rough, jerky, pedestrian, frequently little more than a day-to-day calendar; pages are filled with sentence paragraphs that add to the jerkiness; Grove's obsession with ellipsis marks, a fashion that he took up for a time, is a constant irritation. Then, too, he had an unfortunate tendency toward horrendous foreshadowing, "Something dreadful was coming, coming." And toward portentous inflation: when Ellen and Niels finally do get together for the first time and Niels is about to propose, "the decision was at hand: it was almost oppressive. Some step was to be taken, had to be taken at last: it was a tragic necessity no longer to be evaded" (94). Here, as elsewhere, Grove reduces the word "tragic" to a meaningless filler.

The characters are often wooden and ludicrous, "vague, schematic figures," because Grove's mathematical mind was taken up with equations of his symbolic machinery. Niels's chastity is no doubt important symbolically, but in human terms his adolescence or innocence is so protracted as to border on sheer stupidity. When he gets his house built that he had planned for Ellen after being in love with her for four or five years, he reflects, "But then, here he was sitting on the Marsh; five miles north she was sitting in the bush. How were they to get together?" The reader is tempted to make suggestions. Niels is over thirty when Mrs. Vogel gets him into the park at night: "Intensely whispered came the words, 'Kiss me!' Not knowing what he did, he bent down and kissed her. . . . He had done what he had never done before; he had touched a woman: the touch had set his blood aflame. He almost hated the woman for what she had done to him" (120–21). Clara had no reason to be surprised after their marriage that she still had to make the advances. The symbolic, schematic cosmos that Grove was trying to create did not grow organically from the people nor from the land they lived in.

III   *The Yoke of Life*

Just as Grove first planned his nature essays to be complementary volumes, one of winter and one of summer, so *The Yoke of Life* forms a complement to *Settlers* in the overall movement. As *Settlers* moves upward to life, so *The Yoke* moves down to the death on the lakeshore with the approach of winter. At the same time, it fulfills Book III, "Male and Female," of the original trilogy, "Pioneers." Rousseau's dictum in *Emile* that "It is not good that man should be alone" is here expanded into a larger view of man's incompleteness: "A human being is, in mind and soul, imperfect by itself. ... A half is seeking the other half which will complete it into a self-contained whole" (67). This search for the completion of man and woman is the main action of *The Yoke of Life* as the inner action or theme is the metamorphosis from adolescence to adulthood, a movement in individual history that is a counterpart to the cultural epochs of the human race. It is the metamorphosis that determines the time span of the novel, the seven years in Len Sterner's life from fourteen to twenty-one, a life division, "that septennium of his life in which we establish our whole spiritual outlook" (164). This theme was emphasized in the title that Grove preferred for several years, "Adolescence." Yet a further thematic intention was in the first title that he gave the book, "Equal Opportunities," with its implication of Rousseau's *in*equalities—those created by nature and those imposed by man. The published title, with a different emphasis, also comes from *The Origin of Inequality:* "All gladly offered their necks to the yoke, thinking they were securing their liberty." [5] It is a novel of many theses.

Its method is something that Grove was careful to draw attention to in some very pompous jargon. It is that of "the mythic poets who project into nature the procreations of that awe in which they stand of themselves, in the forms of fabulous concrescences of incongruous parts which they harmonise into imaginable wholes" (68). He is speaking of symbolism.

[84]

The story is divided into four parts that fall into two large divisions: Boyhood, Youth; Manhood, Death. (Grove used these same headings for the four parts of *In Search of Myself*, except that he called Part IV "And After.") The action of each of the two divisions is propelled by a natural disaster, so that here, as in *Over Prairie Trails*, nature is a shaping force in the lives of men. The action takes place from 1912 to 1919, taking in World War I and the beginning of its aftermath, and it concerns the generation following the settlers, so that the main character has not the special isolation of the immigrant which Branden and Lindstedt had. The sense of ongoing time and of development comes with the occasional mention of Lindstedt and his farm and even in the fact that the Lunds are now scarcely remembered. Such is the third part of the Big Grassy Marsh trilogy.

Len Sterner, his younger brother Charlie, their mother and their stepfather, Mack Kolm, struggle to make a living on a debt-ridden farm. A school opens in the district, taught by the aging Mr. Crawford, who has high hopes for Len's future. The other pupil of the same age is Lydia Hausmann, Len's sweetheart. Disaster comes as a hailstorm wipes out the crops on the farm, and at eighteen Len assumes the yoke of family and property, goes to a lumber camp where he spends a winter of "waiterdom" in the kitchens, and tides the family over the crisis with the money he earns. Lydia has also left school to work as a domestic in a nearby village, but when Len returns in the spring, she has turned coquette, scorns the farm, and longs for money and a life in the city. Len vows to become a university professor for her sake, and under Mr. Crawford's tutelage he takes his high school entrance examinations and passes first in the province. When he gets the news, he leaps on a horse and gallops to Lydia —only to find her surrounded by three young men, each of whom in turn she has promised to marry. Stunned and humiliated, Len rushes off. As Lydia escapes to the city in the car of a fourth man, one of her suitors tries to shoot her, kills one of the others instead, and then shoots himself. That is the end of the first division of *The Yoke of Life*.

In the early part of the novel, the sense of the magic world of Romance, of the wonder of the earth is in the imagery. A layer of smoke rising from a smudge pot creates "a witch's habitation in an enchanted forest"; the strange light of a coming storm on a distant upland shows as "an emerald in the black velvet of the forest"; the Lake, some miles off, "was as distant and wonderful as fairyland." After a meeting with Lydia, Len returns to his home, a knight-errant back from the realms of gold: "Since he had left the place a few hours ago, he had sailed the seven seas and been away for years" (77). In Len's forest, a configuration of light, branches, and a small deer take the shape of a unicorn, the ancient symbol of chastity, here emerging from the spring woods as a symbol of human adolescence. At one point, Lydia appears as Miranda, "etherealised, de-carnalised" (178), with schoolmaster Prospero-Grove-Crawford presiding over the brave new world and the young lovers in it. The movement of the first division is the despoiling of that shining world of magic and virginity. It is an exemplum of the opening sentence of *Emile,* which one of the characters paraphrases: "Wherever the world is as God made it, it's glory! Only where man sits down, it's spiled!" (180). It is also, of course, a stage in human metamorphosis. As Len tells Lydia, "While you were at home, you were the pupa. You have burst your shell and become a butterfly" (157). But the natural growth has been warped by contact with society, for Lydia in the village, for Len in the lumber camp. He acknowledges to himself that his love for her has lost its innocence: "as his knowledge of the world widened out, a new, carnal, and jealous element stole into his thought of her" (140).

The second division is the difficult ascent to purging and regeneration, the trial and triumph of the saint whose death is his victory. The pattern has strong similarities to that of *Settlers* and to that of the first quest in *A Search for America*. Once again, St. Anthony is evoked, this time in the prefacing quotation to 'Manhood," from Baudelaire's *Les Fleurs du Mal:* "Où Saint Antoine a vu surgir comme des laves/ Les seins nus et pourprés de ses tentations" (Canto CXI, "Femmes Damnées"; stanza 3).

The division opens with another disaster in what is the most haunting scene of the book. At night, wolves chase Kolm's horses into the quicksand of the swamp. Kolm, the two boys, and a neighbor rush to the place with ropes and lanterns and build a fire so that they can see. The black night and the shooting flames outline the horror: "The very slough seemed to move. In one place, four twitching legs stuck up into the air; in another a horse lay on its side, immersed in the mud but twisting its head upward; that head looked as if moulded of chocolate-brown wet clay" (201–2). Rescue efforts are useless; the horses are sucked down. "They're for the wolves," says Kolm.

Grove uses the scene in two ways. Without horses there is no way to harvest the crop, and so once more Len goes to work to save the family, this time in the city as a teamster delivering coal. But the disaster not only shatters Len's hopes of continuing his education; it awakens in him insight and sympathy. In the horror of the screaming horses with the howling of the wolves in the background, Len sees Lydia's plight—the encircling men driving her to her destruction.

In the city, Len makes fitful gestures at continuing his education at night, but the desire to find Lydia overwhelms everything else, and, wearing his farmer's sheepskin, he begins to keep a night watch on the streets, gradually becoming "gaunt, bearded, hollow-eyed"—the suffering saint. After about a year, he finds her one night in spring. She has become a whore; she is Clara; she is St. Anthony's Queen of Sheba, "centuries old, contemporary with the sphinx and the women of Babylon" (284). Len collapses in a faint which develops into pneumonia, and Lydia nurses him through fever and delirium with the help of a kind doctor. Before he recovers, their money gives out and Lydia takes to the streets to earn their food. One night Len catches her as she is leaving. He then begins plans for their journey to the Lake, the mysterious, magical world of his boyhood dreams, to the purifying wilderness, to redemption, union, and death. He buys a boat, and they set out on the lake, rowing, sailing, camping at night until they get beyond settled areas to the wilderness. Their union, flesh and soul, physical and metaphysical, is consummated; they make a suicide pact; Lydia lights a sacrificial fire of their belongings; they push out in the boat into a storm; Len lashes their bodies together in token of their union; and they drown. At the same moment, of course, inland a son is born to Len's brother Charlie, and so there is the rebirth of life, the resurrection. The child is christened Leonard "as a promise, perhaps, that he should have the opportunities which his older namesake had lacked" (354).

The anticlimax of that closing sentence of *The Yoke of Life* shows the book's main weakness: the plethora of themes. After highly emotional drama about the universe and man, Grove brings us back to the theme that he started with in the first, hand-written version, "Equal Opportunities," with its social comment that Len is denied his self-fulfillment because he cannot get the education that would lead to that fulfillment. On the other hand, he gave up all efforts toward an education because of the overpowering need for Lydia. Both of them were children of the soil and therefore innately good: she had fallen; he must redeem her. But there is another compulsion deeper than any such moral motive. Just as Emile must have his Sophie, so Len must have Lydia, for "Between him and this girl there was an everlasting bond. . . . As in him, there was something god-like in her, different though it might be. And he subordinated himself, not to her, but as a part is subordinated to the whole, the whole consisting of the two of them united. They were equinascent, of equal rights and equal worth; and whether she saw it or not, they fitted together: they formed the possible whole" (165–66). The two bodies lashed together are the two seeking halves which have found each other; and Len's seeking for Lydia was not free action, it was obligatory for his own completion. The bodies are another symbol of the primordial hermaphrodite.

As this thesis takes over and determines the action of the second half of the book, the characters stiffen to puppets and the symbols to dead abstractions. It has no more real unity with the first part than the two bodies have with each other. The book, too, is tied together.

In the Marshland trilogy, Grove pondered several aspects of the individual—the I-not-I or Thoreau's "doubleness," the fixed laws of an individual nature ("Are we we? Or are we products of circumstance?" as Niels asks), the compulsive need of the human being for completion—together with other themes from Rousseau about education, equal opportunities, and the nature of slavery. Such questions occupied the world in which Branden declared Burroughs was coming into his own, a world moving "away from the accidentals of life and towards the essentials," the world of the Romantic tradition. It is the attitudes and tenets of that tradition that Grove superimposed upon the land and people of the Falmouth-Ferguson area, and Grove did less than Rousseau did to shape his two-year experience from 1917 to 1919 among settlers in Manitoba.

CHAPTER 6

Wider Acquaintance

IT WAS only a few months after the first book, *Over Prairie Trails*, was published, that Grove met his two most generous and enduring champions, Arthur Leonard Phelps and Watson Kirkconnell. They met at the Teachers' Convention in Winnipeg in March 1923, where Phelps was giving an address. Both men were young, Phelps in his mid-thirties and Kirkconnell twenty-eight; both were slight and of middle height—their protégé towered above them—both were from the East and recent comers to their jobs. Phelps was head of the English Department at Wesley College; Kirkconnell, who had joined him only a few months before, was the rest of it. Grove was quick to take advantage of his new acquaintances by asking Phelps to write a foreword to the forthcoming book, *The Turn of the Year*, and before March was over, Phelps wrote him in some distress: "Your manuscript is before me. I have enjoyed much of it—have been troubled over much of it—I don't like it as well as your *Prairie Trails*." However, he wrote the foreword, and for several years after Grove depended on Phelps as his literary adviser. He used Kirkconnell as a private library service.

Both men, but particularly Phelps, had a network of connections that had much to do with Grove's advancement. Phelps knew some of the lively young men from Winnipeg who had gone to jobs in the East, such as W. A. Deacon who was literary editor of *Toronto Saturday Night*, and Graham Spry who became the executive secretary of the Canadian Clubs, and he also had close connections with the Ryerson Press, not only because it was the organ of the Methodist church, but because he was a close personal friend of Lorne Pierce, its president, and because in 1922 the press had just published his second chapbook of verse. But perhaps most important of all was Phelps's summer home at Bobcaygeon in the Kawartha Lakes in central Ontario. About fifty yards from Phelps's cottage was that of E. J. Pratt; Hugh Eayrs of Macmillan took up a cottage there in the late 1920's; Lorne Pierce, Deacon, and various others having to do with Canadian letters were visitors. It was among this circle that Phelps passed around Grove's manuscripts. "A name to conjure with, that—Bobcaygeon," Deacon wrote in *Saturday Night*.

In the meantime, the early months of living in Rapid City had been good ones for the Groves: Mrs. Grove started a Wolf Cub Pack; Grove directed a play for the Anglican church; and Miss May Grove recited at the Christmas concert. Principal Grove was once more teaching mathematics and science, frightening girls with snakes, and telling tall tales about himself: deep-sea diving for treasure in the Caribbean, adventures with sleeping bags in the Arctic, experiences on the staff of the *London Times*. "We were aware that Grove romanced. We enjoyed it, but it was pure fantasy. He just told the stories as though he had participated in them. But I never thought anything less of him for telling them." [1] After school hours, the Barrett farm, a couple of miles from town, became a favorite visiting place: "He said he liked the peace. He came often. Came and walked back. I think most of us liked him in school. But he was really strict. You didn't go to him like you'd go to another teacher." [2]

But there are other accounts of Grove's irascibility, his stubbornness, sometimes his outright injustice that explain the extraordinary directive passed by the school board at their November meeting and recorded in *The Reporter*, November 8, 1923: "The Principal was requested to report any case of misbehavior occurring in the high school, to the Secretary, same to be dealt with by the Chairman and the Secretary." On December 11, a special meeting was held "to deal with the resignation of Principal Grove. The resignation was accepted with regret, and the Secretary instructed to advertise for applications for the position." Phelps wrote from Winnipeg: "I don't know whether to consider your letter disquieting or not. . . . Some sense I had concerning your letter made me wonder if the matter would not blow over— as if, after all, you wouldn't be back at work in the school with the New Year. . . . At first I was all for interfering . . . then I thought you'd probably not want such monkeying at all. Is there anything I can do?"

The pattern was repeating itself for a last time—another mid-term resignation. Winkler was the only school where Grove taught for as long as two full years.

But Phelps was right; Grove was back in the school in the New Year. The man who was to take his place proved to be so incompetent that the school board got his "resignation" promptly, and before the end of January they had reengaged Grove to complete his contract year, which ended in June. It was all a bit farcical, except that it left a residue of sourness on all sides.

The next incident involved May. Following the usual custom, the results of Easter examinations were printed in the paper, and they appeared on April 17. The teacher of grade 3 appended a note to her class list saying that May Grove and David Gardner had missed one exam with the result that May Grove's average was 65 percent, David Gardner's 57 percent. On April 24, the paper published a correction: "These pupils missed one examination and were entitled to percentages of 82 and 68 respectively." Thereafter, May Grove's name does not appear in class reports. Her parents took her out of school, and for two years, with permission of the inspector, they tutored her at home. The Groves withdrew further and further from the life of the community.

At the same time, with Ernest Birkinshaw who was gifted in mathematics, Grove showed the generous side of his nature in tutoring him for two years after he had given up teaching. "I had access to his home," Birkinshaw said. "Whenever I wanted to go in there with some problem, I could go in. There was some quality—some warmth there. He was so kind to me. I have a tremendous respect for him."

Grove not only tutored him in mathematics but led him to other interests also. "There was his real interest in Bates's *A Naturalist On The Amazon*—this is a book he told me to buy in the Everyman Library. I've told several people that this was a book that influenced Grove because he thought it was important. That and Darwin's book, *A Naturalist On The Voyage Of The H.M.S. Beagle*—you know, where he did all those studies on that island? The other books he recommended were John Burroughs —I have his *Locust And Wild Honey*—and of course Thoreau, in Everyman. He had quite a library of Everyman books. You know, you could get them for about fifty cents. And this was the library he recommended me to get because they were cheap and the classics were well represented. So those were the books—some of them he gave to me, some he insisted that I buy. But I don't remember any books other than Everyman ones in his home when I used to go there."

At the beginning of 1925, Phelps, who had read and was excited about *Settlers*, which had already been turned down by McClelland & Stewart, was busy planning a hearing for Grove and his work before the local branch of the Canadian Authors' Association. The meeting was to be in early February, when Lorne Pierce of Ryerson's was to be in Winnipeg, but Phelps wrote that if Pierce should not be interested, *"It's just possible that at that meeting we might get enough advance subscriptions to launch your novel,"* and he proposes a *"Reading Recital! !"* The italics reveal his excitement, and no designing mother ever planned more carefully the coming-out party of her debutante daughter. "My suggestion is that you talk, for, say, 20 or 25 minutes on 'My Idea of a Novel,' expanding those thoughts of yours on *Beauty Power Depth*, and then read for half or three quarters of an hour." The reading recital took place before an audience of two hundred; Grove read "Marsh Fire" and "Lost." Lorne Pierce was present, he was maneuvered into reading *Settlers*, and Grove got Ryerson's definite acceptance of it on April 8. The author was launched both at home and abroad.

The quite lengthy report of the meeting in the *Manitoba Free Press*, possibly by Kirkconnell, noted: "Beauty, depth, and power —these were his qualifications for a good novel. He contrasted the short story, the tale and the novel, and came back to the last as the work of his life." This was a fairly remarkable declaration from someone who had yet to publish novel or short story—an aspect of his paper that is not apparent in the version of it in the collection of essays, *It Needs to Be Said*, that Grove published in 1929. There he called it "The Novel." [3] The distinctions that he drew were arbitrary ones without much validity, probably because Grove had limited critical vocabulary. As he sometimes boasted, "I am a man without a formal education" (*It Needs to Be Said*, 49). At any rate, statements such as, "the tale is not *socially significant*," or "Both Short Story and Novel, on the other hand, deal with *socially significant* things from the main stream of life" (the italics are his), are not very helpful and do not mean much even in terms of Grove's own writing. "Marsh Fire," one of the "mere sketches, 'tales from the margin'" that he read to the meeting, for instance, was an episode that had been cut from an earlier version of *Settlers of the Marsh*—a long, loose string of events from which items could easily be detached and published separately, as many of them were. It is this fact, and Grove's practice, that makes nonsense of his categories of Tale, Short Story, and Novel. When is social significance not social significance? And is that a relevant literary measure in any case?

However, the newspaper report, Phelps's letters, and other correspondence give a glimpse of Grove's short stories at the time. In September 1924, Grove had sent a group of them to a literary agent in New York; he sent more in April, and still more the next November. But though the agent tried every publication from *Harper's Magazine* to *Saturday Evening Post,* he could not make a sale, and in November 1927 Grove recalled them. In the meantime he had published a number of them in the *Winnipeg Tribune* which ran a series of his stories and sketches from October 1926 to April 1927, and paid Grove $20 for each item. In 1929 and in later years, he tried to publish a collection of the stories under the title "Tales from the Margin," but without success. It is only recently that they have become available in a collection.[4]

"Snow," which appears in most anthologies of Canadian short stories, has Grove's accurately observed detail, and it has a central figure, Abe Carroll, the leader of men, which was the aspect that Grove first gave to Niels Lindstedt in Book I of the projected "Pioneers" trilogy, and which he later reconstituted in Abe Spalding of *Fruits of the Earth.* Structurally, this story of finding a man frozen to death after a blizzard has the two-part quality of the larger works, *America* or *Yoke of Life,* but here it has a broken-back effect. The focus shifts from the shivering wife with her six children left in a log shack to her parents six miles off and their financial troubles. It is to the parents, rather than to the widow and the children, that the greater emphasis is given, and the story ends with them. As parts of a novel, both of these aspects of human misery would find room, but in the confines of a short story, they draw the reader's attention in divergent directions. There are other incongruities. Two of the would-be rescuers whom the wife has summoned to her home to help, quickly gather her husband's whiskey bottle and a roll of bedding for him, but instead of getting on their horses and riding out to find him, they stand around for two hours in the log shack while a third goes for a cutter. It is a curiously leisurely rescue. All of this might have been clear in a larger context.

Another of the stories in the *Tribune* series was "The Boat," which is set in the Pas-de-Calais area that Grove was so fond of, but which he later recast—and weakened—in *In Search of Myself.* This story is remarkable in comparison with the ones set in Manitoba in that it has none of their awkwardness of phrasing, of character portrayal, or of movement. Its prose is poised, controlled, and polished. It is remarkable that the same person, writing in the same language, and at the same time, should show such variance in the command of that language. Yet the quality of "The Boat" is in the first episode of *Over Prairie Trails* also.

"The Boat" is a boy's journey to the Lighthouse, and although he is forced back by the rushing tide, at last he wins another distant goal—favor in his father's eyes. He lives in a world of Chirico perspectives, "Apart from those white huts, far inland, and the lighthouse which, in a straight line across the water, was now no more than two or at most three miles away, there was not a sign of the world of human beings anywhere" (238). Yet in a moment that world can turn to fury. "The rain lashed the beach; and the wind tore and whirled through the pinnacles of the rocks. I saw nothing any longer of the water; but I heard the breakers rolling in" (240). The boy knows fear and courage and pride. This is one of the best of Grove's short pieces.

Words poured out of Grove in the years immediately after he stopped teaching. It was an anxious time, for he was now committed to the career of writer, and the sense of compulsion must have been as strong as it was in the Winkler letters. As a professional writer he set about trying various avenues that might yield an income. Apart from the short stories, he tried his hand at reviews, particularly in *The Canadian Bookman* which, though it did not pay, did help to make writers known. Grove's reviewing was not generally remarkable, but there is one passage in one of his reviews that is of interest in relation to his own work: "There is a test for the novelist; if the story admits of being transferred from one milieu to another, it had better be told without the sauce piquante of any milieu. Preferable still, it had better remain untold." [5] Grove liked to pontificate, but often it meant little.

One of his experiments in fiction, for instance, was a detective story, which he set in the area around Ashfield north of Winni· peg. But, like *Settlers of the Marsh*, this tale has little relationship with its locale. "Murder in the Quarry" exists in a typescript of 186 double-spaced pages, divided into two parts: "The Crime" (the first hundred pages) and "The Trial." A man is killed in a stone quarry, and the interest of the first section lies in determining the trajectory of the shot. There is a good deal of first year physics and some geometry explained by the police inspector, but then he gets the help of a surveyor, a geologist, and a botanist. The result of all the expertise is that they arrest the wrong man. Part II, "The Trial," which takes place in Winnipeg, is a tedious recounting from the surveyor, geologist, and so forth, of all that they discussed in Part I. On the last page and a half, the prisoner saves himself when he is allowed to cross-examine his wife, who turns out to be the killer. Fortunately, Grove did not try this type of fiction again.

One aspect of the story is worth noting, however, for in the husband and wife Grove has reproduced Niels and Clara. The husband was seduced into marriage while he was drunk, as his wife's mother had earlier seduced the father. The husband feels that his now sexless marriage is a pollution from which he must cleanse himself. Grove's men are a most singularly innocent and marrying lot.

Another experiment, this time set in Winnipeg and Banff, Grove took much more seriously. It was his attempt at James Branch Cabell's manner, and he called it "The Canyon, or The Poet's Dream: A Romance and Its Sequel." In the Author's Note, Grove records his indebtedness for "the thought content of this book"; "a friend sent me James Branch Cabell's 'Beyond Life,' and in it I found some of my own conclusions so perfectly expressed that I oculd not resist the temptation to borrow two or three phrases literally. I herewith make my bow to Mr. Cabell." He borrowed a good deal more than two or three phrases, but among the phrases there is a reference to a supralove of "a life beyond life; and of a death beyond the mere death of a body" (204); there is a paraphrase from Cabell's *The Cream of the Jest* in "it was a fall only since they knew it to be such; that is the cosmic

jest contained in the fable of the tree of knowledge" (222); and
there is a free adaptation of the idea which Cabell expresses in
The High Place: "There is nothing in life which possession does
not discover to be inadequate: we are cursed with a tyrannous
need for what life does not afford." [6]

As an attempt to follow Cabell, "The Canyon" lacks the de-
tachment, the laughter, the comic spirit as well as the variety
of life in any member of Cabell's enormous novel sequence. It is
narrow, tight-lipped, forced, another of Grove's either-or propo-
sitions: "Between spirit and flesh, there is war everlasting" (234).
There is no ground for compromise, no place for humanity, only
an attenuated nervous logic. Since it was being written at about
the same time as *The Yoke of Life,* it throws light on the temper
of the ending of that book also. In the summer of 1925, Phelps
was passing both of them around the Bobcaygeon group, and
on returning "The Canyon" to Grove he wrote, "It made Mrs.
Pratt say she wishes you'd give us another *Over Prairie Trails!*
Ned himself greatly enjoyed the descriptive element, certain situ-
ations, but was dubious over so much analytic cocoon-spinning";
Phelps adds, "I am prone to say that it's too analytic, lacking in
action and human variety to make 'a seller.' "

The story is about Frances Montcrieff, beautiful, wealthy, from
Toronto, who meets Dr. Harold Tracy, professor of English at
Manitoba, who has just published a slim volume of sonnets. Like
Len and Lydia, they are "equinascent, of equal rights and equal
worth," but they are both twenty-six and so beyond the stage
of adolescence; both are orphans, and so there are no troublesome
human ties; both are of equal nobility of mind; both are virgins—
like Niels, Harold's "idealised vision of his mother had kept him
inviolate, so that he had never known temptation." Harold follows her to Banff where they meet again in the mountains: "The
early morning is virgin; in the mountains, all the virginity of
the world seems to be concentrated in that hour," and they have
a moment of high and sexless ecstasy when "their lips met in
chastest of kisses." Two days later they marry, and they feel "as
if they had fallen from innocence." For Harold, "his suffering
sprang from this dualism of flesh and soul" (52); for Frances,
"the biological aspect of sex relations leapt into the foreground
of her focalisations" (81). (For Grove, his prose goes to pieces.)

They return to Winnipeg, but Harold can no longer write, and their marriage begins to disintegrate. They try abstinence, but that does not help, so in a final effort at redemption, they return to the mountains in early fall—they have been married two months—where the weather is "peculiarly chaste, but chaste from abstinence, not from virginity." Unfortunately, a snow storm in the mountains reawakens human emotion, and they fall again. Realizing that "she would drag him down into the dust" (225), Frances throws herself into the terrible vortex of the canyon, the symbol of "the canyon in her through which life had torn its tortuous, writhing path" (211), and thus "the immortal poet's soul in him will live to eternity." Two years later, Harold marries a good housekeeper, and after a number of years he produces two volumes of verse.

There are two or three things of interest in all this in relation to Grove's attitudes. One is that "nature" is taking some very strange turns. Nature is no longer all good but is a vulgarizer of the soul, a biological trap. Not society but nature is the destroyer of the pristine freedom: "Leave it to nature, she thought bitterly, to drag the highest into the dust" (95). Frances's words here throw light on Mrs. Elliot of *Our Daily Bread* as well as on the tortured saints of *Settlers* and *The Yoke of Life*. With all of them as with Frances, sex defiles. The admirable relationship is brother and sister, brother and brother, son and mother.

Another aspect of the male-female relationship comes up in a discussion of the man's creativity and the woman's place in it (81–82). It has echoes of Shaw's *Man and Superman*, but with stronger hermaphroditic overtones. The artist has the long burden of gestation, the pangs of birth; he is the one who is fertilized and who, Frances says, needs fertilizing only once. The artist is the queen of an ant colony, an idea that was certainly in Grove's mind at the time of this writing. The woman too is bisexual. She is not only the female bearer of children and, in Shaw's sense, superman as she protects them and the race, but in this tale she is also the fertilizer, "the occasion *of the phenomenon of love in man*" (165, Grove's italics), and the inspiration, once and for all, of the artist's work. It does not matter that Harold's last book had a period of eighteen years' gestation. Frances lives in it as the fertilizer of it. In symbols, the hermaphrodite has taken the place of the Percheron gelding of *Settlers*.

Grove is obsessed by symbolism in this book. Most of his symbols are commonplace, predictable, and dull, but he constantly points them out: "The leaves were getting brittle. . . . Soon they would turn yellow and fall. All things were symbolic" (100). " 'I wish,' she said, 'we could climb Mount Sulpher once more.' The symbolism of her speech was almost unbearable" (71). "The plains were a symbol to her of the life within the conventions" (165). Like other infatuations, this one is tiresome to the outsider.

As with *The Yoke of Life*, Grove tries to present this story as a tragic one. "The gradual decay of the conception of the beloved being, as reality replaces illusion, is the most tragical thing in the world" (106). "The worst of human tragedies, she reflected, is anti-climax" (216). Once more the concept of tragedy is diminished. Grove's use of the word in these ways reveals his lack of critical equipment and a lack of a sense of proportion, of relative values.

Yet another experiment of these years had to do with animal fable. In the summer of 1924 a book was published that showed the range and flexibility of ant society as the background for "a Satire on the History of Mankind," which was the subtitle of *The Ants of Timothy Thümmel* by Arpad Ferenczy, a professor of sociology and jurisprudence at the University of Budapest. It was published in London, New York, and Toronto, and widely reviewed, though somewhat tardily by Deacon in *Saturday Night*, February 14.

Ferenczy's allegory traced the development of ant society through the rise of parasitic clergy, landholder, and warrior classes, with the subjugation of the workers, until a World Ant War came. Then the workers overthrew their rulers, who were no longer able to protect them, and established a harmonious egalitarian society under a new divine revelation that work is the only title to life. The analogy with World War I and the Russian Revolution is obvious. So are the parallels between the machinery that Ferenczy used for his fable and the machinery that Grove set up for his.

Ferenczy chose for his exemplars the Aruwimi ants, living in a forest glade in central Africa north of the Congo. Grove chose the Atta Gigantea ants living in a valley in central South America, north of the Amazon. The fictional scribe in the one is Professor Thümmel, a renowned zoologist; in the other, F. Philgrove, an amateur myrmecologist. Thümmel deciphers his history in ant tracings on certain leaves, and an ant scholar communicates with Philgrove by dotting letters on a page of his open book. When Thümmel returns home he is put in a madhouse where he commits suicide; Philgrove admits: "I knew I was living at the very edge of the dreamland of insanity."

But apart from parallels on the fictional level there are also interesting parallels in the factual basis. As the *New York Times* review said of Ferenczy's book, "There are no incidents in the imaginary tale that do not find their foundations on scientific data or theory directly based on such data" (August 31, 1924; III, 22:1). And at the end of the book, Ferenczy has a considerable bibliography of literature on ant life which was compiled for him by two (nonfictional) Fellows of the Entomological Society of London. Among the works cited are those of Forel, Latreille, Huber, Emery, and Wheeler, all of whom Ferenczy had drawn upon, and some of whom—especially Wheeler—he quoted. To the names of Forel, Latreille, Huber, Emery, Grove adds Bates on the Amazon and Belt on Nicaragua for suitable geographic authority. He also lays stress on W. M. Wheeler's remarkable book, *Ants, Their Structure, Development and Behaviour*, which had been published in 1910. Indeed, Grove's title is a parody of Wheeler's: "MAN, His Habits, Social Organisation, and Outlook."

The fictional-factual introduction of about sixty pages to what Grove came to call his "Ant Book," remained intact when he completely recast the body of the work in 1933 into what is essentially the text of *Consider Her Ways*, the last of Grove's books to be published in his lifetime. But in this first version, the fiction and the ants soon disappear, except for some awkward footnotes, in a voluminous preachment of over two hundred typed, single-spaced pages that Grove was proud of until he showed it to Phelps, who "knocked the conceit out of me by saying, 'A pretty good sermon, that.' " [7]

Much of this mass of material is an elaboration of the first essay in *Walden*—"Economy"—and of Part II of Rousseau's *Origins of Inequality*, but it also recapitulates the views which Grove had presented in 1914 in "Rousseau as Educator."

Here again are the stages of human history—hunting, pastoral, agricultural, commercial, industrial, intellectual—that Grove used in *America* and elsewhere; the theory from Rousseau and Froebel that the child summarizes these stages, and that the child's natural play will lead to a desire for learning, to education, and to an "establishment of a final harmony with nature" (20–21) which "induction" defeats. Here also is the declaration that agriculture is the highest form of human endeavor and the farmer the most valuable worker of "the world's work."

Grove quotes "Thorough" as saying, "Trade curses everything it handles"; he deplores the economy of nations that is based on supply and demand whereby valuable work or food may become worthless, and he suggests instead that trade be based on wheat as a meaningful standard of value. People living on a rice-based diet might not see the logic of that.

Following Rousseau, he observes that natural inequalities of strength or talent intensified by artificial economic inequalities lead to social inequality and thence to mental inequality, which establishes one kind of slavery. But that is not the only kind of slavery—"Man was born free, and everywhere he is in chains"— and it is essential to recognize disguised slavery of money, of land, of lust, all of which Grove had already exemplified in his books. The way out of slavery as Thoreau and Carlyle had advocated, and as Grove cited in *America,* was for man in general to simplify his wants.

But there is the good wealthy man too (Grove's version of Steffens' good bad man), "The single, enormously rich man is rather apt to be conscience stricken at his own enormous iniquity, and thus, in a futile attempt at expiation, he may devote at least part of his wealth to worthy purposes; to the large-scale endowment of charity or education," which is the motivation of the chief character of *The Master of the Mill.*

The traditional diatribes against privileged sons who become lawyers serve to point up how often Grove fulminates in clichés and how unobservant he was of the human life around him—in this instance, of course, of the Manitoba Law School, which was full of penurious young men from north Winnipeg. What is valuable in this very dull script is that it gathers together and re-states Grove's most enduring convictions, however naïve they may be, which he repeats for most of his life, even after he has obviously grown away from them. It also gives us the intellectual milieu for his characteristic thesis novels.

CHAPTER 7

A Trilogy on Generations

THE MAIN characters that Grove had so far created were for the most part orphans—even Len Sterner was part orphan, for he had lost his father—they had childless marriages, and they were preoccupied with the present. The past was largely irrelevant. This peculiarity served to isolate the particular aspects of human metamorphosis that Grove was concerned with, for his people were not hampered by normal relationships with parents, with brothers and sisters, or with children. The single immigrant lent himself naturally to this isolated condition, and otherwise Grove stipulated it as in the unpublished "The Canyon." The isolation is bound up with the recurring theme of the soul's awakening which, in turn no doubt, has the effect of making Grove's world a sterile, or at least a virginal, one. *The Yoke of Life* is transitional in that Len Sterner's concern for his family ties him to their property slavery, which destroys his own hopes for a different life.

At the same time that Grove was writing *The Yoke of Life* he was also working out, or at any rate contemplating, the theme of generations, the government or organization of the family, and the question of patriarchy and what had become of it. The early volumes of *The Forsyte Saga* had been exciting interest and, though Grove in his letters to Kirkconnell professed to disdain them, they probably had something to do with the direction which his interest now took. Nevertheless, in the shift of focus he was still pondering Rousseau-Thoreau reflections. If Rousseau declares society to be degenerate, Thoreau asks: "But why do men degenerate ever? What makes families run out? What is the nature of the luxury which enervates and destroys nations? Are we sure that there is none of it in our own lives?"[1] It was on this theme that Grove wrote three novels, though only the first was published: *Our Daily Bread*, "The Weatherhead Fortunes," and

"Jane Atkinson." The first two must have been written quite close together, for Phelps had read *Our Daily Bread* by the beginning of November 1925, and Ryerson Press received the manuscript of "The Weatherhead Fortunes" in April 1926. "Jane Atkinson" must have followed shortly after.

Grove's venture into Galsworthy saga is not of one family, but of *the* family in different aspects: the first is the book of the patriarch, John Elliot; the second is the book of the matriarch, Mrs. Weatherhead; the third, the book of the next generation, children of two other families, the Forrests and the Atkinsons. Grove connects the degeneration of the family to an enveloping change in human society, the change from the agricultural to the commercial life, and this movement is reflected in the settings of the books, from the country to the small town to the city. Like the books of the Big Grassy Marsh, this trilogy has interlocking localities and linking figures. Dr. Weatherhead is the figure common to all three. He is an old derelict in his brief appearance toward the end of *Our Daily Bread;* he is the man on the path of failure in "The Weatherhead Fortunes"; and a man in the vigor of life in "Jane Atkinson." The linking locality is Fisher Landing (Grove's name for Rapid City), where Weatherhead lives. Thirty miles south of it is the small city of Stockton, or Brandon, the main locale of "Jane Atkinson." Both of these places are included in the grand survey of *Our Daily Bread,* as the Elliot family spread out from the parental home near Swift Current, Saskatchewan, to southern Manitoba, Winnipeg, Brandon, Rapid City, and British Columbia.

The setting of the partriarchal *Our Daily Bread* is not only the factual landscape of southern Saskatchewan; it is a vision of the elemental, eternal land: "Everywhere the brown, drab earth showed over the bare clay hills" (4); there is "bare hill after hill" on "the flat, treeless, wild prairie" (81). Within this land, John Elliot, fifty-five when the novel opens, has always had two dreams, to raise a large family honorably, and to see "his children settled about him as the children of the patriarchs of Israel were settled about their fathers" (7). He has realized the first of his dreams: "he had lived and multiplied; he had grown, created, not *acquired* his, and his children's daily bread; he had served God" (190). He is the by now familiar figure of the Sower from *The Turn of the Year,* the aged Icelander from *Settlers;* but he is the peculiarly meaningful Sower of both father and farmer, and as the Elliot family stand around the table before a meal and he reads to them the parable from Mark 4, he is conscious of the fusion. Moreover, his wife has been his true mate, the complement of his own nature. Agriculturalist and father, he is the apex of creation, the ideal of human life.

But his second dream, to see "the Elliots of Sedgeby" settled on land surrounding the parental home, "the grey house in the hollow between the hills," to see his children "a re-creation of himself, multiplying his own personality"—Grove's dream of his child in *Over Prairie Trails*—failed, and the book is the history of its failure. Elliot gradually becomes aware that his children are not extensions of himself nor of his wife nor yet a blending of the two, for "in each of them a third thing had appeared, their individual being," and in each that third thing is different from all the others. It is Branden's "I must be I" again. Elliot is puzzled and frightened by the question, "Whence were they?" The foundations of his life are further shaken by his wife who, dying of cancer, turns against him, denounces their childbearing, and condemns herself as the harlot of Babylon. Here is another soul-and-body struggle; sex is a defilement in spite of the ideal union.

Together with the divisiveness of the individual and the riding guilt about sexual life, this world within world is going awry because of the shift from the agricultural life to another cultural epoch. The spirit of the commercial world comes through in a son-in-law who is a swindler, another a petty scrounger, a son who flits from one job to another, hoping always for the big chance. "It's the spirit of the times," an economist says. One by one the children depart from the prosperous farm, leaving their father alone and bitter: "they were rebels in the house of their father: their aims were not what his aims had been" (191). The spacious house, the father's mansion, symbol of his achievement and pride, sheltering, protecting, fostering, becomes now the mirror of Elliot's decay. He shuts off one room after another; when a window breaks, he pastes black tar paper over it. He becomes a miser. But he continues to till the land until he is no longer able to. At seventy-four he rents the farm and starts out to visit his eight living children. "The empty house between the hills of Sedgeby . . . had been left by all who then filled it, even by him" (377).

As he goes from city to farm, from hovel to mansion, his disappointment grows; he can find no "refuge to rest from life." He overhears his children discussing arrangements for him, and he sees himself as "an old, infirm man, of no earthly use. He was in the way. And yet he could not be left alone. That was the worst." He runs away, and over a period of weeks slowly makes his way, avoiding people (an ancient Branden), back to his house where he collapses, unconscious. His children find him in its ruins: "The room in which their father lay was open to the winds."

The ending of the book is moving as the old man's struggles and his visions, advancing together, gather force. But the quality of it is that of the pathos of Wordsworth's "Michael": "The pity which was then in every heart/ For the old Man." It is essentially the Romantic life view.

What Grove had wanted to create, however, was a greater figure than Michael, one that would fit the timeless land. Apart from the implications of biblical patriarch at the beginning, Grove calls on other associations when a son-in-law calls John Elliot "Lear of the prairies!" All that Lear and Elliot have in common are age, querulousness, and restlessness. Otherwise, they are worlds apart. This book is another example of Grove's complaint that he was rarely able to express what he wanted to say, that what came out was not what he had intended. And in general, in spite of the grand conception at the beginning and the poignancy of the ending, *Our Daily Bread* is a mediocre work, most of it on the level of a not very good soap opera of noncredible characters uttering nonhuman dialogue.

But *Our Daily Bread* is only one facet of the theme of family. Elliot believed that the disintegration of the family came because he lost his wife, the completion of the whole entity. Grove seems to agree with him in the title of the first of the three sections, "The Passing of Mrs. Elliot," which is followed by "Chaos." It was she who kept the parts of the family together; patriarchy was not a complete principle of life. Predictably, as part of this thesis, Grove next postulates, not the complement, but its opposite and equally deficient female principle, matriarchy. "The Weatherhead Fortunes," set in the small town of Fisher Landing, is another record of the decline and fall of a family. The setting is irrelevant.

Dr. Percy Weatherhead, son of a former deputy minister of immigration, graduate of Queen's, London, and Leipzig, F.R.C.P., married and moved west after his father died. Like a number of Grove's men, Weatherhead was forty when he began his new life. So far, the pattern is the same as John Elliot's who also married and moved west from Manitoba after the death of his father, though he was then thirty-two. But whereas Elliot's fortunes rose to prosperity, Weatherhead's began to decline almost at once. Now after twenty years, their house, the mansion, a sign of their one-time affluence, remains to mock them, an expensive burden.

Forces beyond their control were largely responsible for their plight. One was local: the railroad had changed its route, and the town, instead of booming, shrank to a village. The other was the spirit of the times. As Weatherhead's young, brash assistant said, "this is a commercial age. Everybody, everywhere, is after money." The commercial world is distorting not only the agricultural life of the country but the professional life of the town also. The assistant sets up an independent practice and ruthlessly takes over Weatherhead's patients and their money. Both Elliot and Weatherhead are anachronisms in the commercial world.

But the Weatherhead fortunes are not only financial. Like the Elliots' they are human and internal, bound to the divisive "I." The old doctor himself says of his dwindled practice: "Perhaps I might have avoided it, if I had not been I. I am of the old generation. I am of a race of men that is gone. My father was not; I am. Where it comes from, I cannot tell " (44). Weatherhead is an earlier version of Sam Clark in *The Master of the Mill*. He echoes John Elliot on the enigma of children: "We live in them, you and I. But there is a third thing in them: their own personality. Whence it is, we do not know. It is there." The Weatherheads create three of these enigmas. The youngest turns into a thief and at the end of the book disappears into the unknown taking with him money from the town hall and the mill, as well as his mother's savings. The eldest, George, is elegant and aimless, one of Grove's perpetual adolescents, overwhelmed by "the *load* of life, the *burden* of life," returning home at thirty-one shabby and penniless and crying to his mother, "Why can't such as I remain children all their lives?" (179). He goes off to live as a hermit, teaching school in immigrant settlements. The other child, Leilah, who left home despising the façade that her mother tried to keep up—"I don't want to be a Weatherhead. The name means nothing to me except shabby gentility and silly pretensions"—makes a successful career for herself in the city. She who rejected the traditional family rescues her destitute parents from Fisher Landing, keeps them with her, and shelters them. She is unmarried, and the family is at an end; in Fisher Landing "the Weatherheads are a memory only". Their history is another of "those domestic tales," like "Michael."

But the focus of the tale is Mrs. Weatherhead, the force of energy in the family, the matriarch, Elliot's counterpart, but gone awry. She contributes to their financial destruction by burning down the sumptuous house, thinking to get insurance from it, only to discover that the insurance had lapsed the day before. She contributes to their moral destruction by having seduced her husband into marriage—not as grossly as Clara did Niels, but just as deliberately—for she saw in it her last chance at social and financial security. And so she must atone to the doctor "for the great wrong she had done him." It is a stony, punitive world that Grove's people live in, harsher than simply an eye for an eye. She contributes to her own destruction through her impossible dreams, her constant idol building, her refusal to face reality. As her husband tells her, "One idol crumbles, you build another. With idols we cannot live." She made an idol first of her husband, then of George, and as the idols fall, she is shattered with them.

Her influence on George is similar to that of the mothers of Niels and of Harold Tracy on them, for "She knew that his feeling for her kept him inviolate against temptations of the coarser kind; . . . she eclipsed the young girls who tried to flirt with him down-town and whom he despised" (30); "She had subtly treated him still more like a lover; had adorned herself for his eye still more like a mistress" (36). If this were another writer, there would be no doubt about the fact that this mother had been destroying her son's life—Lawrence's *Sons and Lovers* had come out in 1913 —but that is not so in Grove. This is another example of the sexless love that he so often presents as an ideal relationship, and George is indeed "a clean man" such as the doctor holds up for admiration.

As Grove tried to elevate *Our Daily Bread* by reference to *Lear,* so, in spite of all of Mrs. Weatherhead's folly, he implies an exalted sphere for her and George by a quotation from Baudelaire: "Par son enfant madone transpercée." This quotation prefaces the story and recurs in Mrs. Weatherhead's delirious vision of a figure with George's face, holding a dagger, who "was sent to pierce her heart" in order to save her and who brought the dagger down "with tremendous force, right into her body and through it, pinning her to the boards of the bier. From the body thus pierced, there issued an agonised cry, and the woman awoke from death" (207). Chaucer's parson would have made good use of this domestic tale, this "moral tale vertuous."

As for the theme of the degeneration of the family and the questions that Thoreau raised, Grove seems to be saying that the family belongs to the agricultural phase of human existence, that it cannot survive in the commercial world, but he also seems to be saying that Rousseau's individual will always destroy the social man, the citizen, and so the family cannot exist anyway, and it never did—witness the conflict of generations from legendary Lear on.

But the family has three parts; he has now examined two of them, the patriarch and the matriarch; there remains only the third, the children. This element is the subject of the last member of the trilogy, "Jane Atkinson."

The main setting is the small prairie city of Stockton, but that city and the main characters have grown out of the Fisher Landing countryside, as the commercial world develops from the agricultural. Yet the novel is set *upon* that city rather than within it, just as, in one section when Jane goes to Banff, the same mountains, lakes, and paths are named as appear in "The Canyon." But here they play no integral part in the action or the theme. This is another thesis novel, in which the author makes moves with schematic figures.

The main characters are the children of two prosperous farm families, the Forrests and the Atkinsons, whose property lies only a few miles from Fisher Landing (Dr. Weatherhead is the families' doctor and in his prime). There are the two Forrest brothers, Arthur and James Alvin, whose dead parents, Isaac and Rebecca, "had some notion of a family place where centuries from now the Forrests would sit and farm"—John Elliot's dream of the Elliots of Sedgeby. On the adjoining farm is Jane Atkinson who, as the novel opens in 1897, has just returned with her bachelor of arts degree from the University of Toronto. The three represent three aspects of human society: Jane, the intellectual world; Arthur, the agricultural world; and Jim, the commercial world—and that world in its most ruthless individualism as his childhood nickname, "I Myself" indicated. He belongs to the great con game. He has been in California and has returned only upon learning that his parents are dead and that a legacy awaits him, and he sets up a business arrangement in Stockton.

Jane and Arthur had been childhood sweethearts, but Jane now falls in love with the traveled and exciting Jim and agrees to marry him. Jim and her father buy and furnish for her "one of the proudest dwellings ever built in the little city." However, on the eve of her marriage, Jane suddenly realizes with horror that marriage had something to do with sex, that it meant "physical intimacy with a man" (78)—a girl brought up on a farm, no less—and on her wedding night she locks herself in her library. The marriage goes unconsummated until she coyly invites her husband into her bed on their first wedding anniversary. Out of the coupling a child, Norah, is born, who grows up a virtual orphan in the hands of a French governess.

Nine years later, Jane is pregnant again when she has an attack of appendicitis and has to have an operation. As she convalesces, she and Jim drive up to the Lake which has its usual cleansing effect. There, for the first time, Jane begins to feel "like a matriarch," and they find a tentative unity. To complete her convalescence, Jane goes to Banff accompanied by her father, where the rarefied atmosphere has as strange an effect on her as it had on the high-minded Frances of "The Canyon."Jane's sense of tentative unity with Jim begins to fade, as "In spite of her pregnancy she felt more and more virgin. She was she, uninvaded by the personality of any other." The sense of matriarchy is completely shattered when a waitress working in a Banff hotel reveals that she, too, is Mrs. James A. Forrest, but that she has priority and a twelve-year-old son. Jim's marriage to Jane was bigamous, and so there is no family at all.

When Jane returns to the sumptuous mansion she gives Jim house room, but they do not communicate. She tells him: "the mere legal entanglement is nothing to me. . . . But you were impure." It was not what he had done, but what he *was* that Jane rejected. This is the logical dead end of the "I must be I" notion of the individual following the determined rules of his nature. A virtuous man, like Niels, may fall and return to himself, but a wicked man cannot become other than he is. For Jim, as it had been for Clara Vogel, death was the only way out. After eight or nine years, having lost all his money, he commits suicide as the only way of redressing the situation in which he had placed the two women. (It was a leisurely decision.) At the end of the book, Norah is about to get a divorce so that she can marry a man who also has to get a divorce before the marriage can occur. This is the rubble that is left of the traditional family.

As with the other two parts of the trilogy, Grove tried to elevate the level of this tale, this time by the frequent—and loose— use of the word "tragic." For instance, Jane reacted "more deeply, more passionately than the average person, and therefore, her destiny could not but be tragic" (4). When she becomes infatuated with Jim, "she was in love, hopelessly, tragically in love" (55). When she wakes in the library after her non-wedding night, she wakes to "the tragic reality: she was in her husband's house!" (91). When Jane confronts Jim with his bigamy, "The way in which he exposed what she considered his crudity impressed her as out-right tragic" (184). The misapplication of a word, however, does not exalt the fatuous.

Jane and Arthur, now in their fifties, resume their childhood love affair; agriculture triumphant, they live on the adjoining farms in twilight happiness, untroubled by sex, which Jane had considered "an imperfection in the scheme of things" (154). The impression grows that Grove's people might be in paradise on this earth if only nature had not thought up the distasteful device of genitalia, if man had been fashioned like Raphael's cherubs. Jane and Arthur are a final comment on the trilogy: No patriarch; no matriarch; only two virgins—no family.

Something else is emerging, however. The pregnant Jane, in a preview of artificial insemination, was confident that "she was she, uninvaded by the personality of any other," and a few months later Jim Forrest reflected bitterly on "that house of his in which, as he knew, an infant, a boy, was going to be raised as if the birth of children were parthenogenetic" (196). This virgin mother, together with the once-only-fertilized poet and the ant queen, implies a society in which the family has been superseded. The human race is shifting its biological organization.

Another matter that becomes increasingly explicit in the novels of these years is Grove's deep-seated dualism. It is present in his tortured saints—Branden, Niels, Len—and personified in the Ellen-Clara contrast. It is stated of Harold Tracy—"His suffering sprang from this dualism of flesh and soul"; and it is rephrased by Jane—"she had not distinguished between what, in her love, might be physical, what spiritual. Now this dualism was extremely disturbing" (68). There is a strange contradiction here with the Rousseau tenet that man is innately good, that there is no original sin in the human heart, for Grove's Manichean dualism predates original sin, which implies choice and action. Grove's good and evil are absolutes.

CHAPTER 8

Controversy and Desolation

GROVE'S first novel, *Settlers of the Marsh*, was published in September 1925.

On Tuesday, January 5, 1926, a paragraph much smaller than a man's hand appeared in the "City and District" column of the *Manitoba Free Press:* "Aldermen Condemn Modern Novels. In the opinion of Ald. F. H. Davidson and A. H. Pulford, many modern novels are trashy and prurient, and the buying of them should be cut down by the public libraries of the city, incidentally diminishing the library expenditure. Several books were mentioned by the holders of this opinion, among them being a few prize novels of the past year."

Two days later, the *Winnipeg Tribune* took the matter up obliquely by strongly objecting to the Ontario government's proposed legislation aimed at "preventing lending libraries from supplying fiction of the type generally described as salacious," and observing that "Censorship of books invariably leads to the very evils it aims to destroy. It is invariably directed, too, at the wrong authors." On Monday the *Free Press* had an editorial on "Aldermen And The Public Library," apparently quoting verbatim aldermanic opinion on current fiction: "they think it is the bunk. Also it is punk. As an expression of opinion, this is of no particular interest; but it becomes of interest when these views are put forward as reasons for curtailing the appropriation of libraries."

Then the excitement moved abroad. *Bookseller and Stationer,* a monthly publication of the Maclean Publishing Company, in its March issue gave further details: "Among the fiction offerings which experienced the storm of the City Fathers' condemnation were Ralph Connor's 'Treading the Winepress,' Fannie Hurst's 'Mannequin,' and Martha Ostenso's 'Wild Geese.'" Interestingly, Grove and *Settlers of the Marsh* were never mentioned, though the Reverend Gordon (Ralph Connor) was. At some point in the excitement, Phelps wrote an undated note to Grove, apparently in late January, saying, "The library has banned the *Settlers* and Eaton's sell it—*but quietly!*" The hot line to Toronto thrummed and Deacon sounded the call to arms on February 13, in a piece entitled, "Muzzle The Native! ! !" Everything was getting thoroughly confused now. Deacon declared: "Grove's 'Settlers Of The Marsh' has been banned by the Winnipeg Public Library. Miss Ostenso's 'Wild Geese' has not. . . . Why is not 'Wild Geese' banned too? Can something be done to the local man, which cannot be done with impunity to the expatriate?" The censorship controversy widened with the publication of Dreiser's *An American Tragedy*, and in his column of April 17, Deacon writes, "Congratulations to the Ottawa 'Journal' for its sane and sound editorial on book censorship. Has no one else the simple courage? I am glad to hear that the Toronto police have banned Theodore Dreiser's 'American Tragedy.' The book (in two volumes) costs $15, and is the greatest piece of imaginative literature to come out of the U.S. in a decade. It sadly needed this advertising to overcome the price handicap; and now it will be popular." Deacon's fight for the right was only too worthy, but he took some overly free swipes, one at Professor Allison, book reviewer for the *Winnipeg Tribune*, who was instrumental in getting the paper to accept Grove's short stories and sketches. Deacon claimed that Allison had said that *Wild Geese* was "prurient and ought not to be in free circulation," and that *Settlers* was "scandalously immoral." The following week, Allison being on vacation called on Deacon, and on June 12 *Saturday Night* reported that Allison had written that he considered the novel *Wild Geese* "one of the most brilliant ever written in Canada, but . . . unfit reading for a 16-year-old girl"; that he thought *Settlers* "the much bigger and finer and stronger thing, but he objected to the free circulation of this even more on grounds of the decencies."

The free and wide-ranging comment naturally interested librarians, and the librarian of the Calgary Public Library wrote privately to the librarian of the Winnipeg Public Library on June 19: "The March number of the Canadian Bookseller & Stationer printed an editorial regarding some criticisms of Winnipeg aldermen regarding certain novels, including Treading the Winepress & Wild Geese. I am rather curious to know whether they sought to put any pressure on your Board to ban these books and what final action was taken regarding your estimates. This censorship question is likely to become rather critical in Canada in the next few years." The Winnipeg librarian, J. H. McCarthy, replied immediately:

In explanation I wish to say that the remarks of these aldermen were never made seriously. They were chatting informally in the ante-room and expressed these remarks with a carelessness and with a sense of irresponsibility that would not have been the case in the Committee-room or in any other official way. They were not speaking for publication and were more put out about the publicity than anyone else. It was never brought up officially in the Committee-room or elsewhere to my knowledge.

There has not been the slightest attempt for many years to ban any books that have been put into the library and my estimates for books were passed with very little deduction and with comparatively little discussion. In short, the incident was magnified, the remarks were not made thoughtfully nor seriously, and, as is usually the case, there was all the more flurry about it.

Settlers had not been banned. Neither had any of the books that the aldermen *had* mentioned. But the story persisted for many years. Unfortunately, the publicity did not help sales, and *Settlers* was a financial disappointment for both author and publisher.

In view of all this, however, it is not surprising that there had been shocked sensibilities in Rapid City. One of the students of the time, now a matron of a hospital, said, "at the time that they were in Rapid City, *Settlers Of The Marsh* was published, and this was a terr-rible book, people were horrified that there should be some sex in this book, you know. And of course, we were forbidden to read it, and of course we did everything we could to get to read it." [1] No doubt *Settlers* added a further grievance to others that had been accumulating among certain groups in Rapid City.

On April 8, in the same issue in which *The Reporter* announced, "An Essex 'six' coach was delivered at F. P. Grove's on Tuesday," there was a disquieting note in the account of the monthly school board meeting: "The Secretary was instructed to request that Mrs. Grove kindly furnish the report for grades 6 and 8 for March." This action apparently followed upon the March report from the principal of the school that had been disturbing. Again in May, the school board instructed the secretary "to write Mrs. Grove stating that the Board would appreciate reports of tests to be made as suggested." Obviously, there was friction within the school.

Early in June the storm broke. A petition "for the dismissal of Mrs. Grove from the teaching staff" was sent to the school board by the Returned Soldiers' Organization. In the minutes of the school board meeting "all trustees being present and E. S. Gardiner in the chair," the secretary was instructed to acknowledge receipt of the petition and to say "that after giving said petition careful consideration and in view of Inspector Hartley's written report supplemented with his verbal report, both of which were highly commendable to Mrs. Grove, we feel that we would fail in our duty if we acceded to their request." The motion was moved by Cooper Stone, editor of *The Reporter,* and seconded by Ernest Birkinshaw. It carried.

On June 17, a letter appeared in the paper from W. E. Barrett, at whose home the Groves had been such frequent visitors, defending them and revealing the contents of the petition:

I wish to say a few words regarding the ungentlemanly action of a few persons acting under the name of the Ret. Sol. Organization in submitting a petition to the School Board, parading their own virtues and asking the removal of Mr. and Mrs. Grove from the neighborhood on the grounds that they believe these people to be Mennonites; that their ideals and mode of living do not conform to what a Canadian's should be, that they do not send their own child to school (which is supposed to be part of the Mennonite creed, that they shall not submit to compulsory education); that they do not believe in warfare; that they are disturbers of the peace; and that they are not the people who should help to mould the lives of the boys and girls in their care; and that so long as they remain in this neighborhood they (the petitioners) cannot maintain the peace they fought and bled for, etc. . . .

Now as to their child not going to school I beg to differ. She did attend school but was taken from it, as was also the child of the present board's chairman for certain reasons, most people know why. She is receiving private tuition which has been OK'd by the inspector.

Now as to the lives of our young being moulded by such people. I take pleasure in stating that four of our children have been under Mrs. Grove and if we are all here I hope to have four more.

[114]

There is a wry turn in the fact that Grove is now accused of being a Mennonite and undermining children by spreading Mennonite doctrine, while in Winkler he was accused of undermining the faith of Mennonite children by teaching non-Mennonite doctrine.

The muddle of accusations shows an accumulated sense of injury and resentment beginning with the causes that led to Grove's resignation from the school, the hubbub over the grade 3 standing of May Grove and David Gardiner, the present friction with the new principal, the moral disapproval of *Settlers*—together with wounds from Grove's cruel tongue which spared no one. But all of it might have remained only as bad memories—as it did with many in other localities—had it not been caught up in the bitterness of war's aftermath.

Ernest Birkinshaw, Jr., musing on how the whole thing could have come about, said: "A little community like Rapid City had sent a lot of boys, and a lot of boys had been killed in the war. And then a lot of these boys had gone over and they had fought Germans, and there was a terrible anti-German feeling in the community. And Grove, with his rolling of r's—he sounded like a German. And he said things that made him sound as though he were sympathetic to the German cause. My father defended Grove, but you know, he'd say he was a fool, that Grove was a fool, and I think most people in a community that size would think he was a bit of a fool in some ways. He brought this antagonism on." [2] An active movement began to get Grove out of the community, and in the current school principal, a veteran and an officer, the movement found a leader.

One day Mrs. Grove asked Mr. Birkinshaw to come to talk with her husband—"the only time I was ever in his house although I knew him so well; it was a sort of sacred cow; he didn't invite you there so we didn't go there." The school principal was a mason, and Birkinshaw was a mason: "Grove had got it into his head somehow that everybody who was a mason must be against him—and despite all that I could say that day—he was sobbing there like a child—I couldn't do anything with him." [3]

But if the malcontents had found a leader, the spirit of the little town had a leader, too. The school board stood firm. It stood firm against the powerful emotional pull of the returned men, "and Grove was a hard man to stand firm for." Barrett's letter to the paper was the voice of the sense of justice and dignity of that small town, but there was action, too. Other papers were circulated, and on June 21, the school board was presented with seven pages containing 158 signatures of ratepayers saying: "We the undersigned desire to express our approval of the action of the school board in re-engaging Mrs. Grove as teacher of Grades 6 and 8." Another petition was also presented, with 70 signatures on it and saying, "We, the pupils, ex-pupils and intending pupils of Mrs. Grove's room, humbly beg the School Board to maintain Mrs. Grove's services for another year." And Grove, a man not given to expressing gratitude, wrote a letter to the editor:

Sir: I cannot leave town, even for a holiday, without thanking our many friends for the courageous and effective way in which they have downed the dastardly attack from the dark, and around a corner which has been levelled against a defenceless woman: defenceless because unskilled in the use of underhand weapons; her only crime being that she did her duty unflinchingly and unremittingly with somewhat more than the usual devotion, and therefore, with somewhat more than the usual success. . . .

We have agreed to return to this town. We have done so under the pressure of public opinion; our own inclinations would have led us to seek greener fields. But we felt that it would be ungrateful indeed not to listen to the plea of those who have shown themselves to be our friends, especially since their number proved to be so much greater than, in our most optimistic moods, we should have expected.

In the same issue, "Local News" reported that the Groves were leaving that day in the new Essex for a holiday trip to British Columbia and California.

In September, May returned to school. But by mid-September Grove was in bed with a disability that seemed to be akin to sciatica. He went to the Brandon hospital, but the doctors seemed unable to diagnose it. He returned home and was bedridden until December, when the paper reported, on December 23: "We are pleased to report F. P. Grove now able to be out again, with the aid of crutches. Mr. Grove has been confined for over three months." Meantime, Deacon was keeping *Saturday Night* subscribers informed with bulletins on Grove's health; Kirkconnell was running a shuttle service of books to and from Rapid City;

and Phelps was interesting Winnipeg medical men in Grove's case. On February 6 Phelps wrote that a friend of his would like to help by enlisting specialists whom he knew. "He has asked me if I could get from you the formally stated report of the Brandon men on your case. He would like to present it to his friends here and get their professional advice, free of cost to you of course." Arrangements were made for Grove to go to Winnipeg during Easter, and apparently the doctors suggested an operation on his back, to take place in June. On June 9 Phelps wrote again about plans for Mrs. Grove and May to stay with them while Grove was in the hospital. But the Groves became evasive and, to the puzzlement of Phelps—and no doubt of the doctors—changed their plans. On June 30, *The Reporter* noted that the Groves "left by Auto on Tuesday to spend a few days at Morris, after which they will visit Winnipeg."

May had passed with honors, Mrs. Grove had been reengaged at a slight salary increase, and her sewing class had received acclaim in provincial competitions. The two highest in the class, Bessie Greig, grade 8, and May Grove, grade 6, were the winners of a free trip to Winnipeg, as *The Reporter* recorded with some pride.

On July 21, on page 4 of *The Reporter* was the note, "Mr. and Mrs. F. P. Grove and daughter returned to town last Saturday." On page 8 there was another item:

OBITUARY: As we go to press the community is shocked and deeply grieved over the death of Phyllis May, the eleven year old daughter of Mr. and Mrs. F. P. Grove, which unexpectedly occurred last evening at Minnedosa Hospital after an operation for appendicitis.[4] The funeral will be held from the parents' home on Friday at 3:30 p.m.

Phelps conducted the funeral service.

On August 1, Grove wrote Kirkconnell, who was in the East: "You will have wondered at not having received word from me for so long. Many things have happened. For various reasons my operation was postponed. Instead, my little girl has had to undergo an operation for appendicitis and died under the ether. Since then we have been homeless; and only yesterday had we the courage to face matters here. I am still exceedingly taken up with the various matters arising from her death. They seem to be a last link. Apart from that our own lives are extinct. I am sure you will forgive our taciturnity. Nobody can quite understand what this means to us."

CHAPTER 9

The Canadian Nation

TOO MUCH of our news is coloured and distorted, before ever it reaches the Canadian press. Too often our convictions are borrowed from London, Paris, or New York. Real independence is not the product of tariffs and treaties. It is a spiritual thing. No country has reached its full stature, which makes its goods at home, but not its faith and its philosophy."

Such was part of the opening statement of *The Canadian Forum*, "a monthly journal of opinion," in its first issue, October 1920. A few months earlier, the same spirit had led to the forming of the Group of Seven painters; a few months later, it led to the founding of the Canadian Authors' Association. All of them were part of the creative movement that stirred Canada throughout the 1920's and into the 1930's, and that included a national railway, the United Church, the National Research Council, and eventually the Canadian Broadcasting Corporation. It was, in part, a human answer to the destruction of the 1914-18 war; it was an affirmation of a unity that was born out of that common ordeal; it was a reexamination, from the perspective of that unity, of Canadians as a people and of Canada as their land; and it was a reexamination of the relations of Canada to other countries and of Canadians to each other. It was a nation, now fifty years old, taking pride in itself.

One of the small parts of the general movement was a publishing venture, The Graphic Publishers of Ottawa, begun by H. C. Miller and some fellow enthusiasts, to publish Canadian books, only Canadian books, and only for a Canadian market. It was Miller who accepted the twice-rejected *Search for America* in November 1926 and who brought it out in October 1927. It was Grove's one great success.

Graham Spry, a Manitoba Rhodes Scholar and the newly appointed executive secretary of the Association of Canadian Clubs, learned of the book first while he was visiting in England, from a British Labour M.P., "and I bought it at once and read it, and out of that came Grove's tours for the Canadian Clubs." [1] The Association, which had existed for many years, had recently issued a restatement of its aims, among which were: "To foster and encourage a national public opinion and spirit, to stimulate intelligent citizenship, to awaken an interest in public affairs, and to cultivate an attachment to the institutions and soil of Canada; To foster friendly and equitable relationships between the two great races of the dominion; . . . To assist New Canadians in becoming part of the life of the Dominion; . . . To encourage the study of the arts, literature and history of Canada; its economic organization and its problems generally, and its tradition of British justice and liberty." Toward this end, the association organized clubs across the country, and it arranged speaking tours of writers, artists, and other public figures, as a means of linking the widespread people as well as giving them a chance to know what was being written and painted and thought about Canada. It was into the pervasive intellectual, artistic, political, and spiritual ferment of Canadianism that Grove was drawn with the publication of *A Search for America*. Here was an ideal subject for the Canadian Clubs—an immigrant who had tried life in the United States, spurned it, and chosen Canada; a New Canadian who could give voice to the silent strangers, who could reveal their needs, trials, and dreams to their would-be helpers; and a Canadian writer who had written a fine book—in fact, who now had four books to his credit.

Back in his office in Ottawa, on January 30, 1928, Spry first cautiously wrote to Phelps, whom he knew, asking if Grove was a speaker as well as a writer. If so, he would be glad to arrange a lecture tour of the clubs, and it "would materially assist in making his books known." Spry's letter arrived in Winnipeg at the same time as one to Kirkconnell from Grove, who was himself pondering lecturing possibilities, saying that he wanted to go out and meet people but that he had to make the meetings pay. Spry's letter was a happy coincidence. The arrangements were made for a tour of Ontario with sixteen lectures spread over a month, to begin in early March, fee $25 a lecture with traveling expenses paid, and to be followed by a western tour in the fall for ten weeks. For the first tour, Graphic Publishers and the Canadian Clubs split the $400 for the sixteen lectures, and Graphic supplied two thousand folders to send out to advertise the tour, Grove, and *A Search for America*. [2]

With some temerity at first, Grove embarked on this venture on February 27. The lecture that he had prepared was "Nationhood," which he later published in both *The Canadian Nation* and *It Needs to Be Said*, and which included the sentence he was so very fond of, that with variations appeared in *America*, in *Turn of The Year*, in *Settlers*, and in *Our Daily Bread*: "I take it to be a desire inherent in man as born by woman to own that bit of land whence, with tentative mind, he reaches out into the dark mysteries which surround him." Otherwise, the lecture contained a castigation of materialism and a large dollop of anti-Americanism. Both went well.

Grove soon found that he was a good performer, and on March 3, from Port Arthur, he wrote to his wife: "the hall was small enough so that I could save my voice for the big effects. . . . When I came to the statement of what I found in the west, there was applause after every sentence, then breathless silence, then the thunder again. . . . Financially I believe it will be our salvation. All these people who now know me will want to read my next book too." It was a triumphal tour, and when he arrived in Ottawa shortly after, cloud-capped towers were in his eyes. And they had dollar signs.

At a banquet given by the central executive of the Canadian Club, Spry introduced "the distinguished author of *A Search For America*" as the guest of honor to the company that included Senator Hardy, Honorable Martin Burrell, military men, bank managers, Miller of the Graphic, and editors of the Ottawa papers. Grove wrote home, "I was told that *over 100 Million Dollars* were sitting at the board," and, about two days later, "I have many and powerful friends at Ottawa." He was entertained at a luncheon by the American consul, invited to tea by Lady Pope, and taken out by Woodsworth and his group, "the left wing of the left side of the House of Commons. . . . I never realised quite so forcibly before what a power I am myself in the land." Dreams of a prosperous future were irresistible. "These people here think I should be entitled to an income of 50 to 60,000 a year! ! !" On a more modest scale, some had suggested "a job in the Department of Immigration, and failing that in a college as a professor of moderns or classics." At the regular meeting of the men's Canadian Club, "they told me it was the most brilliant gathering that had ever assembled for any speaker. . . . When I entered the banquet hall, the whole Assembly rose and cheered. . . . Half a dozen times thundering applause during the speech. When I finished, I had to stand fully ten minutes bowing to their applause and their cheering." He was invited for a Sunday to the country home of a multi-millionaire, E. C. Grant.

Leaving "this world of diplomacy and politics and wealth and after all, real culture," Grove stormed the intellectual world in Toronto. As a kindness to his friend Phelps, Pratt had invited Grove to stay with him on his way through to western Ontario towns, and he invited some friends in to meet him: "Had a delightful time with Pratt, Fairley and Alexander in Toronto over the week end," he wrote from Kitchener, March 26. He had also met Hugh Eayrs, president of Macmillan of Canada, and he had sold him two books, *Our Daily Bread* and "Adolescence" *(The Yoke of Life)*. He had arranged with Carrier Publishing Company of Montreal and New York for the American edition of *America*. All things were going well.

When he returned to Toronto for his engagement with the Canadian Club there, the tour ended in a blaze of glory: "Newspaper men stood lined up when the train pulled in, to interview me. Photographers clicked their cameras." He was put in the York Club, "This is the most exclusive club in Canada; it looks down on the Rideau at Ottawa as newly rich. . . . On my arrival ½ hour ago, a valet was placed at my exclusive disposal; and he promptly unpacked my baggage, hanging everything up, etc." For the luncheon meeting, "All my friends (Pratt, Eayrs, Edgar, Alexander, Hutton, Fairley and many others)" were at the head table with him, and the meeting was a great success. "Between 4 and 500 men went frantic over my address." He was not only a powerful public speaker, the swayer of men in the mass; the most reputable literary minds of the University of Toronto hailed him as a writer: "They all know that the rest of Canadian writers are pigmies by my side; and they say so. Alexander, f.i., and Fairley, and others." Canada had recognized Frederick Philip Grove.

Two small avenues, each holding promise, opened up that spring. In February, Graham Spry had brought out the first issue of *The Canadian Nation* as the organ of the Canadian Clubs, "a publication which interprets the Canadian scene in all its variety, through article, short story or sketch," and he paid Grove $50 for a short story, "Drama at the Crossroads," one of the Big Grassy Marsh stories, which appeared in the second issue in April. Also in April, Macmillan sent Grove his first assignment as reader for them, which Eayrs hoped might lead to further editorial work.

At the end of June, *The Reporter*, having recorded the re-engagements of teachers for the next term (Mrs. Grove at $1,350) also noted the Groves' departure "on their annual summer auto trip," this time going East. It was a serene basking in the after-glow of the great tour, staying with the Millers in Ottawa, arranging with Spry for the fall tour and a later one in eastern Canada, meeting Carrier in Montreal and agreeing to do a trans-lation of a German study of Sun Yat-sen, going on to the lovely valleys of the maritimes, back through Niagara Falls, staying with the Eayrs at Bobcaygeon till mid-August, and then home. In the next few weeks, *Our Daily Bread* was published; Carrier brought out their edition of *A Search for America;* and on September 9 Grove started on the western tour. It had been a satisfactory summer.

The western tour, of course, was a disappointment. It could not be anything else. For one thing, the novelty had worn off. As he wrote from Vancouver, "last spring, today's meeting would have excited me, and I should have wired. Now it leaves me quite cold—just like Kamloops: there they nearly carried me to the train." But he is not known, either. In one place, "they in-troduced me as Frederick Philip *Cook*"; in Victoria, the book-sellers did not know his work; in Edmonton, no reservations had been made for him, and "There is not a copy of my book in town"; in the Peace River country, the car ran out of gas on the way to Grande Prairie; and in Prince Albert, though he had a good meeting, he lost his cane.

The lecture act had become tiring. "But it's got to be done. When I've covered this country from coast to coast, I should have enough readers here to support us modestly; and that's what we are aiming at. The frills must come from the U.S.A. I do hope they will come." A week later, "The more I see of this country, the more clearly do I realize that without some such stimulus as this lecture tour, it would take decades longer for my books to penetrate the dense resistance of these people." The tours then become the only way "you can throw up your job in the near future." But since that would not be for a while, he did not buy her the evening dress that she wanted. She would not be needing it for the coming winter.

By mid-November Grove was back in Rapid City, borrowing books from Kirkconnell, working on "Abe Spalding," and translating the book on Sun Yat-sen. At the beginning of the year, an interesting proposition came from Graham Spry. Would Grove be an associate editor of *The Canadian Nation,* which had been enlarged? Spry said that he was asking Marius Barbeau, the French-Canadian folklorist, to be the other associate editor, while Spry would continue as general editor to cover political and economic subjects. "There will be no pay except for whatever work you do for us," but Grove would be in charge of prose and poetry. Grove accepted with pleasure and then started off on his six-week eastern tour.

Montreal renewed the glamor and excitement of the Ottawa triumph. "Montreal was terrific. But I *did* sell books. I must have made $100 in addition to my fees." He also placed with Carrier the manuscript of a remittance man that he had met in British Columbia during the fall tour: "Nobody has ever come to my help like that. Phelps of course. But he did not have the power which I, after all, have now." In the maritimes he found: "Just now I am distinctly 'popular' and that helps sales . . . I don't want to make concessions. I am I. Take me or leave me. That's been my attitude. But . . . how about the money?" Back in Ottawa Grove worked with Spry, "knocking the initial number of the new Canadian Nation into shape," and it appeared in March with the masthead: Graham Spry, Editor; Frederick Philip Grove, Associate Editor; Marius Barbeau, Associate Editor. It included "The Meaning of Nationhood," by now well known across Canada.

But the cloud-capped towers had dimmed a little. Senator Hardy was now suggesting a government job at about $3,000. Two days later, "the premier and Senator Hardy were in conference yesterday; and it was resolved to try to create a job for me at $2,000, *without work.*" Otherwise, Eayrs had indicated further editorial work for Macmillan, and Spry had suggested the possibility of getting a wealthy club or a wealthy patron to subsidize Grove's editorial work for *The Canadian Nation*.

With his usual tendency to translate suggestions into guarantees, Grove wrote home in mid-February, "If I take the job with Macmillans, it will mean that, as far as Canadian things go, I'll be supreme head of the dept. Most of the work I could do at home in the evening. *You* could do a good deal of it: reading MSS etc. I'd get about $200 a month and certain fees—a bread-and-butter job. Royalties would all be extra. I could also go here and there to lecture occasionally. In addition, I'd have a few hundred from *The Canadian Nation*. Only if what the Dominion government may offer me is an absolute sinecure—i.e. pay without work—I'll take it. I do consider that Canada owes me a living."

CHAPTER 10

The End of a Decade

B Y mid-1929, the gaunt towering figure of a man on a platform was in the public eye from coast to coast, and the man had a Voice. Grove saw himself as John crying, "Repent ye!" and indeed he did prick the consciences of his audience, but they were also comforted, for after all this splendid, articulate specimen from Europe had chosen Canada.

Leaders in the literary movement not only rejoiced in the candid social criticisms of the New Canadian, they also saw in him the fulfillment of their dream-vision: this man was the writer they had longed for, who either had produced or was about to produce, but at any rate, had the capacity to produce, The Great Canadian Novel. This dream, of course, was of the jewel that was to crown the whole Canadianism movement. Grove is scarcely to be blamed if he believed them.

Certainly no other book written in Canada before or since received the accolades, the fanfare, the extraordinary publicity that *A Search for America* received. Its radiance shone on the other books that Grove published—now five of them: *Over Prairie Trails,* 1922; *The Turn of the Year,* 1923; *Settlers of the Marsh,* 1925; *Our Daily Bread,* 1928; and in March 1929, *It Needs to Be Said.*

This last is a potboiler of eight pieces, the longest of them the "Nationhood" lecture that appeared in *The Canadian Nation* in the same month. Otherwise, "The Novel" is the paper that Grove gave in Winnipeg in February 1925, at the meeting so carefully arranged by Phelps, in which Grove set up the "socially significant" category; "Realism in Literature" is an expansion of a talk that he gave to the Canadian Authors' convention that summer, the essence of which he later published in a letter to the editor of *The Canadian Bookman* in November 1925—realism apparently meaning whatever Grove happened to like in literature

—and some very short pieces, "The Happy Ending," "The Aim of Art," "The Value of Art," fragments of the sort that he told Kirkconnell he wrote every once in a while and kept by him, which support the impression that Grove never destroyed anything he wrote. The first essay, "A Neglected Function of a Certain Literary Association," is the only one that is relevant to the original title of the volume, "Addresses Not Delivered," and to the footnote on the first page. It had been written for the Canadian Authors' convention in Vancouver in 1926, but social functions had crowded it out. The paper is windy, the pose that of the elder statesman talking down to his audience (surely a little premature in 1926), speaking of "your meeting," "in your ranks," "what you should do"; generalizing expansively about the difference between the spirit of Britain and of the United States in their literatures, and saying some pretty silly things, such as that there is nothing of note in United States literature "since Hawthorne, Thoreau, Emerson have been dead." In some of the other pieces, of course, Grove takes on the role of the plain, blunt man of "no formal education," whose wisdom does "not flow from profound systematic study or prolonged research"; whose reading in literature has been "exceedingly limited"; who declares "I am an autodidact." Whichever role he assumes, it is a self-complimentary one.

It was probably the combination of generalized commonplaces, strutting manner, and florid style that made B. K. Sandwell remark in *Saturday Night*, June 15, "one is impelled to question whether Mr. Grove does not overstate it, whether he does not pitch his trumpet note a little too high." The title that Sandwell gave to his review of *It Needs to Be Said* was, "So Do Some Other Things," and among those things, "The fact is that sincerity, while a very important element in a writer's character, and one which needs to be urged upon Canadians, is by no means sufficient to produce great writing." He called Grove "a writer with a stern artistic conscience" which had led "to the remarkable wide-spread personal admiration for him that has grown up in Canada within a short time." And he continued, "I do not think it would be amiss to say that Canadians are more deeply impressed by his personality than by his work." He concluded his review by agreeing with Grove that Canada needed a great poem more than a great gold mine, "but this volume will not tell us much about how to produce it or how to recognize it when produced." By the end of July, Eayrs said in a letter to Grove, "*It Needs to Be Said* has rather badly flopped."

During those months, Grove had been working on another novel. He wrote Kirkconnell in May: "I am plugging along and have nearly finished a fourth version of my 'Abe Spalding,'" and by July Eayrs had read the completed script and wrote back, "I don't think that Abe Spalding, Pioneer should be cut." It did not appear, however, until 1933, and then it was published by Dent under the title *Fruits of the Earth*.

Like *It Needs to Be Said*, it is a kind of summary of themes and objectives in Grove's work of the decade. The title calls up Mark 4, that John Elliot was accustomed to read before meals, and also Rousseau's declaration, "You are lost if you forget that the fruits of the earth belong equally to us all, and the earth itself to nobody." [1] But the body of the novel—what it is about—was better described by an earlier title, "The Chronicle of Spalding District," for as Grove told Kirkconnell, the idea of the growth of a settlement still excited him—the idea that he had begun with in the original *Settlers*. This time he started with the first man, the one who began a settlement with his homesteading, Abe Spalding, Pioneer.

In the character of Abe himself, Grove presents a summary, a gathering together, and yet an extension of earlier work. Abe is the focal man, the one others look to for help and leadership, a figure presented tentatively in an early version of Niels Lindstedt, that appears in the short stories of the Marsh, and that is in John Elliot in his prime. Abe is also a development of the figure of the sower. He is no longer the humble old man, the servant of God in *The Turn of the Year*, nor Sigurdsen in *Settlers*, nor yet John Elliot. He is an evident power in the lives of other men and of society, an industrial force, the farmer as master. Physically he is an enlarged version of the broad-shouldered men of middle stature—Niels, Elliot, Atkinson—who were the builders of the earlier novels. Abe Spalding is a giant, "a huge figure of somewhat uncertain outlines, resembling the hero of a saga" (85),[2] a symbol of the Paul Bunyan type for the champion against the elements, the conqueror of the vast land, the creator of life and human habitation and of the cities and towns which, if they did not rise out of the prairie an exhalation to the sound of music, had their own miracle in them. In the second part of the novel, this figure dissolves into another: Abe is not the conquering hero, but "the rustic harvest god" (228), as he stands atop a gigantic haystack, grassy weeds and barbs sticking in his hair and eyebrows. The saga figure, "loved by few, hated by some," has mellowed to a beneficent deity.

The change of symbols reflects the twofold nature of the novel, first in its two divisions, "Abe Spalding" and "The District"; then in Abe's inner development from individual to citizen, a development already made familiar in the metamorphosis of Phil Branden; finally in the double vision of that development in the social macrocosm, the phenomenon of the growth of the community, and the movement to government by man, the political animal. In each of the two parts, scenes of voting are the focal high points. "Democracy means putting the right man in the right place," one character says, and Abe himself "was ready to sink his personal wish in the general will. So far, democracy was a reality to him" (161); but defeated, he declares, "I'll tell you what your precious democracy is. A system devised to keep the man who stands out from the common crowd down to the common level. That is all" (168). Like Achilles, he sulks in his tent until scandal and grief strike in his own home and he acknowledges his social responsibility, "The district was calling" (263).

It is no doubt this emphasis or perspective that Grove was referring to when he implied in the Author's Note that he had found a new subject matter that differentiated this book from the "Jane Atkinson" group. Otherwise, the string of events that leads to this development in Abe forms another of Grove's loose, linear narratives in which the years go by like beads on an abacus.

Abe comes not from Europe but from Ontario; and he settles not in the forbidding country of the Marsh but in the rich, open farmland of the area where Grove first taught in southern Manitoba. The year is 1900 and Abe is thirty. His passion for acquiring land makes him not a master but a slave to the land, consuming the years of his own life and those of his wife and their four children. He helps others who settle around him, but only because, "I need roads; I need cross-ditches . . . I'll need a school. That's why I need neighbours." His honesty and shrewdness are recognized by the others, and he is made chairman of the school board and then reeve of the municipality when it is formed in 1912. That is the year of Abe's great crop gamble; he makes $40,000 and builds the mansion, the granaries, the magnificent barns with milking machines for the cows, the chicken coop— all run by electricity. The great night comes when the electricity is to be turned on, and Abe drives off across the bald, flat prairie to get a view of his creation; it blazes forth, a light to lighten the darkness, his Heorot. "That was the proudest moment of his life; and he raised an arm as though reaching for the stars" (119).

The over-elaborate mansion is not the home his wife had wanted for years, and she is out of place in it. Charlie, the eldest child, the one person whom Abe was close to, is killed in an accident for which Abe is culpable. Degeneration sets in: "The moment a work of man was finished, nature set to work to take it down again" (134). It is in the weathering of the bricks, the crumbling of the mortar in the huge house, and it is reflected in the district as the greedy, the corrupt, the vicious begin to invade it. Politically, Abe is defeated and humiliated. His family drifts away; his elder daughter marries a city lawyer; his son leaves the farm for a garage business; the remaining daughter gets pregnant by one of Abe's married farmhands. His great estate with its surrounding trees becomes a lonely fortress against the world of men. To combat the corresponding chaos that has taken hold in the outer world, men of the district appeal to Abe to resume his leadership, to return to the council and the school board. Abe agrees. His own grief has made him partake of others' grief. "True resignation meant accepting one's destiny; to him it meant accepting the burden of leadership; . . . here was something to do once more. . . . He had lived to himself and had had to learn it could not be done" (264).

The twofold aspect of the novel is not only in the chaos and order contrast, or in Abe the individual as against Abe the social man; it reveals itself also in other of Grove's familiar themes. The dualism is in the shift from an agricultural age to a commercial one, a theme which Grove explored in the generations trilogy, and which is in his early and his continuing concern with cultural epochs. It is also in the generation struggle, though Abe is left with his own independence and purpose in life even though he, like John Elliot, had failed in creating a patriarchy. There is the dualism of man and woman in the estrangement of husband and wife after physical attraction "had died in satiety" (a state declared inevitable in "The Canyon"). The two people live as strangers, he for his work and she for the children, their parallel lives not touching until grief establishes at least mutual respect. And there is, of course, the dualism in Abe's change from material values to spiritual ones as he comes to question his life, at which point there is some talk of "cosmic" views, though they do not emerge very clearly. Structurally, the twofold aspect is a reversal, a looking-glass repetition: where Abe wins an election by one vote in the first part, he loses by one vote in the second.

But just as the occasional paragraph suggesting "cosmic" views does not create that sort of dimension in the novel, so what seems to be an attempt at making the prairie into Egdon Heath dissipates after the set piece on the landscape (135–38), which has strong echoes of *The Return of the Native:* "In the particular section where Abe's life as chronicled here unfolded itself, a traveller might, at the time, have gone in an east-west direction for a hundred miles without finding the slightest change in the essentials of the landscape." There is also an attempt, after Hardy, to show a people formed by an environment, though the settlers of the Spalding district had scarcely been there long enough to find out what the environment was: "If they have lived here for some time, a decade or longer . . . so that the landscape has had time to enforce in them a reaction to its own character, they seem slow, deliberate, earthbound. In their features lingers something wistful; in their speech, something hesitating, groping, almost deprecatory and apologetic; in their silences something almost eloquent." The rest of the novel shows that up for the nonsense that it is. Here again, Grove was at his common pastime of trying to impose a literary notion that he had come across upon a new environment, as he had done when he became fascinated with Cabell. He was an eager literary opportunist.

While he had been revising *Fruits of the Earth*, Grove had not been unmindful of his editorship in *The Canadian Nation*. The May–June issue contained another of his short stories, "Salesmanship," but he had been casting about for other contributors, and he wrote Kirkconnell asking if he had any original poetry, "short, to fill half a page," or any striking translations from Ukrainian or "some other language spoken in some 'foreign' settlement," or if there were any book with a Canadian bearing that either he or Phelps would be interested in doing two-thirds of a page on. He went further afield, too. In May, Macmillan sent Grove a manuscript to read, "Here Came a Mortal," by Mrs. Ella B. Wallis of Calgary, and Grove took the somewhat unusual step for a reader of getting in touch directly with the author, giving her his criticisms of the novel, suggesting that Macmillan would possibly not take it, but asking her to send short stories or articles to *The Canadian Nation.* He also wrote to Marcus Adeney, a cellist in the Toronto symphony who had been writing reviews for *The Canadian Bookman,* apparently suggesting that Adeney conduct a page of book reviews for the *Nation* and that he lecture, presumably to Canadian Clubs. Adeney answered with gratitude that he would certainly send an article to the *Nation,* that he had "long wanted to have a hand in the control of some sort of printed sheet," and that while he had "not yet spoken in public" he had no objection to doing so. These two correspondents took second and third prizes in the Graphic Publishers' Literary Competition that Grove conducted in 1930–31, but for the moment their hopes were dashed along with Grove's editorial ambitions. The central executive of the Canadian Clubs decided in the summer of 1929 that the *Nation* was too expensive. They were losing money on it, and since publication was hardly their field anyway, they could no longer support it. The May–June issue was the last one.

About mid-June, Grove wrote a dispirited letter to Kirkconnell: "I have done well last year; but there seems to be an end to it. . . . I am tired of uncertainties. I am nearly 58 years old and want to look forward to a few yrs—if they are vouchsafed—of quiet, settled life. It seems that Canada has nothing to offer me. There was talk of a salary in connection with lectures for the Canadian Clubs—of a sinecure at Ottawa—of editorial work for a publishing firm. Of all this nothing has come. I have a few thousand dollars in the bank (don't mention the fact); and I have 2 or 3 books ready for the press. And so we are discussing the advisability of definitely leaving the country and going where I can make a living. Mrs. G. has done her share; but I won't accept that any longer. . . ."

Toward the end of July, however, a letter came from Eayrs that contained a hope, and an enticing hope, saying that there was a likelihood of an important reorganization in the Canadian Macmillan company, and "I may buy this business entirely. If I do,

[132]

I'll ask you to join me. If I don't I'll likely be able to make a proposal to you to come here and work editorially with me. I know the situation is urgent from your standpoint. All I can say now."

The Groves began to pack. Grove sold his books in Winnipeg, "some 200 vols.," for $38, he wrote Kirkconnell, which since they were nearly all Everyman volumes and some second hand to begin with, was not a bad price, and freight on them would be more than they were worth. On August 29, *The Reporter* noted, "Recent new autos in town include an Essex for F. P. Grove and a Ford for Dr. I. K. Gilhuly." The new Essex was well tested: "we are going to take a steamer trunk, 3 suitcases, club-bag, hat box, portfolio, and a huge bundle of bedding in the car." For October, Currelly, the curator of the Royal Ontario Museum, had generously given them his cottage near Port Hope, so they had an address to go to. On September 9, they drove up the east hill of Rapid City, past the cemetery, and on to begin yet another new life.

PART III

The Book World

CHAPTER 11

Publishers

IN mid-April 1929, less than seven years after Grove published his first book, a somewhat rueful letter from Louis Carrier, who was licking one or two wounds of his own, gives an idea of the tangle that Grove had managed to create among his publishers:

> Rumours are flying thick and fast as usual in the book trade, and many of them concern the prototype of Phil Branden. He has definitely accepted a job as editor for the Macmillans of Canada. No, that is quite wrong; he has accepted a job in Ottawa. That may be so, in any case, he is signed up with Macmillan for his next book. And that cannot be true because all rights for his next book are in the hands of Jonathan Cape, including American and Canadian rights.
>
> Through it all, and much more, we still keep alive the hope that ADOLESCENCE may be placed in our hands for publication say, in the spring of 1930. Is there any chance of acquiring some reliable news, something that is not mere conjecture?

In May, Carrier added another note: "There is no trade as gossipy as the book trade and your name seems to have come in for more than the usual amount of gossip due probably to the fact that you are one of those rare authors who have books published over the imprint of three or four houses." As Carrier suggests, there can have been few authors, in Canada or elsewhere, who were as tenderly wooed by as many publishers as Grove was.

Like the archetypal champion, it is true, he had a slow beginning. McClelland & Stewart did accept *Over Prairie Trails* in December 1919 for publication "next autumn," and it did not appear until October 1922. The interval was filled with letters about rising costs of paper and manufacturing, a strike in printing and binding shops, an offer to release Grove from his contract if he could find another publisher, unsuccessful attempts to ensure sale by appeals to western departments of education, and the ever-present problem of Canadian publishers trying to find United States and British copublishers to "reduce the initial cost." Once it did appear, McClelland & Stewart had the rare experience of a letter from Grove saying that he was "delighted" with the book's design. More than that, it sold far beyond their hopes, and they brought out a second printing in the fall of 1923.

Meanwhile, they had been coaxing this author to send them the script of the companion volume, *The Turn of the Year*, which he had told them about in January 1920. They did not receive a script until two years later, January 1922, and then not in publishable shape. They returned it for revision and more letters followed: in March, they are glad to know that Grove is revising the script; on April 9, glad to hear he is working on it; on April 19, glad to hear there is progress on it. A year later, they received the revised manuscript and sent Grove a contract on May 16, 1923. On May 31, in answer to a letter from Grove, they wrote saying that they could not tell him when they would be sending him proofs. The book was on sale by November, but this time Grove did not like its appearance, and, besides, his name was misspelled on the cover. The book did not sell.

Of Grove's other books, McClelland & Stewart refused the large, uncut version of *The Search for America* in 1923. The publishers also refused the first two parts of Grove's proposed trilogy —*Settlers*, in January 1924, and "The White Range-Line House" in March 1925—as appealing to only a small audience and therefore not likely to be commercially successful. Their correspondence with Grove was resumed briefly in the fall of 1928, when he was arranging to turn over to Macmillan the copyright of his first two books. They agreed, after some bargaining, to sell him their remainders at less than cost, but they added, a little stiffly: "We have been in business for over 21 years and we have played the game fairly with everyone, whether customer, friend or foe, and we do not propose to do anything different at this time. We would much sooner overpay than underpay an author. . . . We do wish that there could be a more kindly feeling between us but somehow your letters to us seem to breathe an atmosphere of threat. . . . We will always feel that we played some part in the launching of your book career in that we had the privilege of publishing your very first book. It is true that we declined some of your manuscripts, but we did so with the opinion that it was in your best interest not to publish these manuscripts as submitted to us at the time. We even hope that some day we shall have the privilege of again having you on our list with a new book." That was the end of McClelland & Stewart during Grove's lifetime.

He sent the rejected manuscripts to Macmillan, which also refused them, and at the behest of Phelps turned his attention to Ryerson, where Lorne Pierce had little joy of him. This time, the trouble began after publication. The early part went smoothly enough: Pierce accepted the manuscript of *Settlers* on April 8, managed to get Doran to take it in the United States and to do the printing, and by mid-July forwarded the proofs and manuscript together with Doran's note: "Please ask Mr. Grove to answer all the printer's queries and to return the galleys and manuscript to us." But when the book came out in the fall, Grove did not like Doran's jacket; he did not receive his author's copies; he said "the book swarms with misprints"; and he found the reviews singularly unintelligent.

In mid-February he wrote Pierce, "I have had a veiled offer from another Canadian publisher who wrote me that in his opinion I was 'now entitled to link up with a publisher who will build me up as an author of succeeding novels.' (I might mention, by the way, that it was Macmillans.)" This sort of thing drew from Pierce a letter that would have abashed most people: "I am sorry that *Settlers Of The Marsh* has been such an unhappy undertaking for you throughout. From the time the Ms. was accepted until the present it seems to have brought you little pleasure." But Grove seemed intent on striking out at someone, to make someone suffer for his disappointment at the reception of the book, and late in April he wrote Pierce accusing him of sneering at Phelps's favorable review of it, of deliberate unkindness and, apparently, of incompetence. Pierce replied on April 28, "Your letter has been very painful to me. . . . Possibly you do not know that Phelps and I are extraordinarily good friends"; and with great patience he ends, "In conclusion let me say that if my letters have seemed 'outright unkind' it is a fault I have to be misunderstood, but let me assure you again, as regards yourself and your work, I entertain the highest of warm regards." Relations were very edgy throughout that spring, although Grove submitted three novels to Ryerson: *Our Daily Bread,* which they were trying to place in England (Harper's, to whom it had been sent at Grove's request, had turned it down in the United States); "The Canyon," which they had sent to Viking who had returned it within a week; and "The Weatherhead Fortunes," which Grove sent them in April.

There was a lull during the summer, with only a sad little note from Phelps: *Settlers* had not gone well: "I feel somehow that it is my fault." But October began with a shriek of outrage from Grove. He had just received, forwarded by Ryerson, the first royalties from Doran. It was a postal note for 90 cents, which he returned to Ryerson. Grove had fallen into the trap of author's corrections. Letters went back and forth; Doran said they had paid their contractual 10 percent of the printer's bill for corrections and that the rest was a clear charge against the author; the Ryerson business office, answering Grove's persistent accusations, wrote: "We are not going to carry this controversy any further. As far as we are concerned your stand in this matter does not meet with our approval. Your statement that the corrections which you made would not amount to more than $1.00 is absurd. The printer's charge for this work is at the rate of $3.00 an hour." On January 21, Pierce wrote a disenchanted farewell: "I have also learned in a roundabout way that you have a book coming out with the Graphic Publishers in Ottawa, your autobiographical manuscript, I believe, which I so much enjoyed reading. I trust it greatly enhances your standing in Canada, which already is considerable."

The last letter from Ryersons about *Settlers* is dated April 21, 1928: "We have your letter of April 17th in reference to royalty on 'Settlers Of The Marsh.' . . . We gave no statement in the fall of 1927 as there were so very few copies of the book sold. . . . There was no desire on our part whatever to evade paying the royalties due you." There was no further communication between Grove and Ryerson for over ten years except for a note to Pierce in 1936 in which Grove reprimanded him for reportedly saying that *The Yoke of Life* was "a pale imitation" of *Jude the Obscure.* No reply was filed.

Two down. The next one up was the unfortunate Miller of The Graphic Publishers of Ottawa with whom Grove signed the contract for *A Search for America* in January 1927; he promised publication for May 1 and he did publish it in October of that year. The Graphic Publishers, beginning in October 1925 with the publishing of *The Land of Afternoon*, a satire on Ottawa society, had become incorporated on July 9, 1926, with H. C. Miller as president. One of the directors was Lawrence J. Burpee, secretary of the International Joint Commission, who had just been elected president of the Royal Society of Canada and who had already written or edited a considerable number of books on Canadian literature and history. Another director was Mrs. M. H. W. (Holly) Cameron, a monied woman in her fifties, president of the stocks-and-bonds company of Cameron-Solmes, and a descendant of old Ottawa families on both sides. She was to supply financial planning and support. By the fall of 1926, Graphic was offering a list of twelve books, and the future looked promising.

Grove's involvement with Graphic and Miller was a Bobcaygeon effort of that summer when Deacon was spending his vacation in Pratt's cottage and Phelps had "this cartload of Ms, wtih him and was bound I should read it." [1] Deacon was impressed, and after Phelps had arranged Grove's agreement to submit it to Graphic, apparently at the end of October, Deacon sent the script to Miller with a note, "Publish this." But in the spring, Graphic's troubles began to brew. Mrs. Cameron had sold shares in the company through the various branches of Cameron-Solmes, [2] and some of the largest shareholders set out to take over the company and to oust Miller, which they did at a meeting held on August 31 when they also established a new board of directors.

Miller tried to cover the turmoil in his letters to Grove by excuses about a new type face not arriving, special paper being delayed, an audit being taken. In June, in answer to Grove's request for an advance on royalties, Miller wrote that he would send a check for $500, but it never arrived. With this following on the 90-cent postal order from Doran, Grove grew understandably discouraged and exasperated. Then in July, May died. When Miller finally did write at the beginning of September to explain the mystifying silences, to Grove the squabbling over control of Graphic sounded distant and trivial.

To Miller it seemed like the end of his dream. However, fortune was in flux, and other directors—original ones and supporters of Miller—defeated the intruders and reinstated Miller as president by September 16. Burpee wrote to Grove in support of Miller, saying that "the Board not only treated him very unjustly but acted very unwisely in the interests of Graphic." The storm blew over for the moment, and Grove's book appeared in bookshops in October—after all, only six months after it had been promised, which was not and is not extraordinary in the book trade. And of course, after *A Search for America* was published, the glory trail began.

Up to this point, Grove had dealt with one publisher at a time. Now he began to play with both hands.

The first matter to come up was *Our Daily Bread*. At the end of 1927, Mrs. Grove wrote Macmillan offering it to them for fall publication. They accepted enthusiastically in mid-February. In Ottawa two months later, Grove wrote home that Macmillan would be the beneficiary of all the publicity while "Poor Miller will, of course, be either furious or mortified when he finds I have given 'Our Daily Bread' to Macmillans. Of course, I'll say it's all *your* fault. The book is yours." He also told her that he had sold Eayrs "Adolescence" *(The Yoke of Life)* "provided he can pull off international publication." Relations with Eayrs were warm: "I have enjoyed Mr. and Mrs. Eayrs very much. They are really delightful people," and they invited the Groves to visit them at Bobcaygeon in the summer.

The other arrangements that he made during the first tour were those with Louis Carrier for the United States and English rights to *A Search for America*. Carrier's firm was another fledgling publishing company whose initial offering was noted by *Saturday Night* on February 4, 1928, only a few weeks before Grove signed a contract with them: "They will publish Canadian and foreign books in both the English and French languages, and will maintain Paris and New York offices as well as covering the entire Canadian trade—English and French—from their head office at Montreal." Friction between them and Graphic had begun by the end of the summer, when Carrier wrote in some concern, asking Grove to confirm the English market where they had a reciprocal arrangement with Brentano's "and issue further orders to the Graphic Publishers to refrain from supplying the English trade, or from sending copies to English papers for review."

About this time, Eayrs began to grow cautious. *Our Daily Bread* came out in October; he promised to do a book of essays,

It Needs to Be Said, in the spring, but he was becoming alarmed at a possible glut of Grove on the market. He began the 1929 New Year with a warning: "As a matter of purely publishing wisdom it is never wise to crowd an author. We had *Our Daily Bread* last Fall, with *Search For America* still going on handily under another imprint. We are doing *It Needs To Be Said* this spring, and we are doing *Adolescence* next Fall. It really gives with *Search* four Grove titles in a year. . . . It is so easy to overcrowd a market, particularly such a small market as Canada is." It was good publishing policy and excellent advice for a young author, but Grove was conscious of time's winged chariot hurrying near, and besides, Carrier was anxious to publish another book by him. From Montreal, on his eastern tour, Grove wrote his wife on January 29, to parcel up a carbon copy of "Adolescence" and send it to Carrier. "I am going to play Carrier against Eayrs—Eayrs against Carrier. I am learning a thing or two."

But that was not the only ball of wool that he let loose. During Grove's lecture visit in Montreal, Carrier took advantage of the excitement and the publicity. "Carrier is, of course, selling his edition here. *I connive.* He is at present selling hundreds of copies a day." The Montreal sales had not—or not yet—affected Graphic, however, because when Grove returned to Ottawa from the maritimes, he was pleasantly surprised by Miller's royalty statement of 1,036 copies sold: "I secured his cheque which I shall forward to the bank as soon as I can. . . . This Miller statement is by $150 better than I had figured with. Not bad. He begs for another book. Well, we'll see."

Things were warming up, and the spring of 1929 was a lively one. Though the dreams of great wealth had dissipated over the preceding year, still there were several prospects that Grove recounted in letters home—the government sinecure, the paid editorship with *The Canadian Nation,* further lectures, the readership with Macmillans—all or some of these would provide a modest but steady month-by-month living. Anything beyond that must come from royalties on his books, and so he must now drive the hardest possible bargain: no more 10 percent royalty agreements, and on the other hand freedom to accept the highest bid offered him.

Carrier wrote that he wanted "Adolescence" very much, that he would publish it in the fall in three countries, would send a contract, "with whatever advance you required," and "if you will consider our offer to publish the book, we are prepared to close immediately." Grove had already written home: "There will be a battle when I reach Toronto, that is sure. Well, I'll be armed."

The first skirmish with Eayrs took place over the telephone on February 18, with Grove refusing to sign the contract for "Adolescence," denying that he owed Macmillan any loyalty, accusing Eayrs of trying to bind him "hand and foot" so that he could not take advantage of other offers, and declaring—so he wrote Mrs. Grove—"I'll offer you my future work; but I won't sign even to that; and I'll make my terms. If I can get better terms elsewhere that's where I'll go. If I deprive myself of that possibility, I make myself your slave." They hung up. Eayrs phoned back to say that he would have the contract redrafted.

The main engagement took place in Eayrs's office. Before leaving his hotel room, Grove started a letter home: "of course, I'd rather stay with Macmillans. I rather think we'll come to terms. . . . I want my freedom, I want a *good* contract for Adolescence, if he wants it. I think I'll try to get Adolescence out in England before it appears here." Back in his room that evening, he finished the letter: "The battle is fought and *won.* . . . We were sailing close to a break for an hour or so. . . . At last he said 'Dictate to me what you want.' And at 5 o'clock the thing was settled—after a battle of 1½ hours." Eayrs's signature on his letters changed from "Most affectionate regards" in January to "Yours very truly" in March, but the "affectionate regard" was back by the beginning of April. Grove had just written him about "a big new novel," Abe Spalding, Pioneer.

Meanwhile, a little to the east, the Carrier-Miller tangle had been proceeding apace. By the beginning of March, they were suing each other over the Canadian sales of *Search*. "Bad news, that. That is, Miller, though quite friendly is suing me to protect him in Canada; and I shall have to sue Carrier. That will probably settle Carrier's friendship." Two weeks later, Miller wrote Grove, now at home in Rapid City, to thank both of them, "for your joint effort of the 11th, enclosing your contract with Carrier . . . we now have definite proof that he is selling 'A Search For America' promiscuously throughout Canada, and we are starting action today."

Mid-April brought the Groves the long and wryly disillusioned letter from Louis Carrier: What about "Adolescence"? But in addition to that, he had received notice that he was being sued and so he had gone directly to Ottawa, had met with the lawyer, Miller, and two of Graphic's directors and had

offered to give them any particulars they required as to the sales we had actually made. I also pointed out that last fall Miller had . . . suggested that we carry the SEARCH as well as other Graphic books, his edition of the SEARCH being carried through Canada concurrently with our own. At the time he had boasted that he had sold more than 200 copies in the U.S. and had raised no objection to my own announcement that we would carry our edition in Canada to even up for his American sales.

My only concern at this stage is the fact that the Ottawa lawyer in his letters seemed to be under the impression that he was representing you as well as the Graphic. His first letter is headed "Frederick Philip Grove and the Graphic Publishers vs Louis Carrier & Co."

I am wondering if you have given him authority to act for you and whether it is your intention to join hands with the Graphic people in any possible suit. Could you let me know your attitude in this respect?

Carrier observed that "The net result of the Ottawa conference was a draw. I do not know yet whether the play-off will be arranged for later on." But in May he wrote, "Graphic seem to have abandoned any idea of sueing us with regard to the SEARCH. They are well advised to do so as I am afraid they would cut a very sorry and ridiculous figure if they did." That seems to be the last letter from Louis Carrier to Grove. The firm folded about a year later; it had existed for approximately two and a half years.

As for Miller, the last letter from him is dated July 25, when he sent a royalty check, regretting that it was not larger: "I hope and trust that Carrier's is much greater as we feel despite his assurances, that his entrance into Canada before the sale was prohibited has seriously damaged our sales and the consequent return to you." The man who had actually published *Search* and who had helped to plan the great tour triumphs got little reward. At Graphic the dissatisfied directors won. On October 31, 1929, The Graphic Publishers Limited was supplanted by a new company incorporated on that day as Graphic Publishers, Limited.[3]

L. J. Burpee, president, and Mrs. Cameron were continuing directors from the earlier company. Miller was out of the firm.

The manuscript of "Adolescence" was still not free from shifts of direction. In spite of the agreement won from Eayrs in the great struggle of February, Grove tried the game of publisher-pitting again, and in October he sent the manuscript to Graphic, following that up by sending them "Abe Spalding" late in November. By this time, Grove had written to Kirkconnell that Toronto offered nothing. "As for Eayrs, I am through with him, though I may publish another book or so through Macmillans. He has broken every promise he made to me." It is possible, of course, that the great stock market crash had altered Eayrs's plans. At any rate, the only further correspondence is about "Adolescence," for which Grove signed a contract in January 1930, and in April changed the title to *The Yoke of Life*. Whatever words passed between the two men at this period were apparently irrevocable. Grove did not approach Macmillan again, after the publication of *The Yoke of Life*, until after Eayrs's death in April 1940.

CHAPTER 12

The Publisher

IN the late fall of 1929 at Bobcaygeon, where the Groves had gone still with no definite prospects after they left Currelly's cottage, they received a letter from Mrs. Cameron urging them to visit her in Ottawa: "This is a little matter between just you, your good wife and myself. I have a proposition altogether apart from your Manuscripts that I wish to discuss with you. I am enclosing a cheque for One Hundred Dollars, so that monetary conditions will not delay your visit." The visit resulted in Grove's joining the Graphic firm in December at a salary of $3,600.

Graphic was in its fifth year of operation, and with the re-incorporation of October 1929, it had moved out to property owned by Mrs. Cameron and her family, the Wolfes, at Eastview along Riverside Drive, an area also known generally as Overbrook. Both Eastview and Overbrook were used as names for different Graphic activities, just as Miller had earlier told Grove that they were preparing Carrier's American edition of *Search* "under the name of the Laurentian Press Syndicate." When Grove joined Graphic, a further division was formed, but unlike the others, this one was formally incorporated on April 1, 1930, as Ariston Publishers, Limited, "with head office situate at Eastview, Ontario." On the list of directors, Grove came first; Burpee was also there, as was Mrs. Cameron who was named vice-president. No one was named president, though Grove had certainly understood, and so had others, that that was his title. Among "Leaders in Public Life, Society, Business and the Professions," of the *Ottawa Journal*'s report of the ceremonial opening of Parliament on February 20, Grove appeared as "President and Editor of the Ariston Publishers Limited, Ottawa."

And so he returned to the dream city which a year and a half before he had called "this world of diplomacy and politics and wealth and after all, real culture." But the lionizing days were over. Grove found himself in a work-a-day world. As Graham Spry reflected, "A thing that was perfectly usual in Ottawa—there are people in the Canadian Club and in official life, who are just constantly seeing people, and there is a sort of network. And while you're making speeches and so on, the network looks after you. But if you come back and settle down, you're just one of the rest of us. And so when Grove came back, the E. C. Grants and the Lady Popes of the world were entertaining the next visitors. And this, after all, for any capital, or any big city, for those who are in this game, is just normal. But I think he felt that very deeply." [1]

And indeed he did. Ten years later, in a bitter letter to Lorne Pierce, Grove burst out, "in Ottawa, I lived in an isolation comparable only to that of an Antarctic explorer. . . . How many of the Ottawa writers called on me or on my wife? Did Scott? Did Burpee? Did anyone? No, not one. It is true that, as an employee of Graphic, I met a few who expected me to print such of their work as they had failed to place elsewhere—Macdonald, for instance" (April 1, 1940).

The bitterness came more from the difference between the dream and its reality than from the possibilities of the life itself. Wilfrid Eggleston, then Ottawa correspondent for *The Toronto Star*, recalled, with the aid of his diary, that he and his wife were invited to tea March 15, "to meet Graham Spry, Mr. and Mrs. George Pepper, Pegi Nichol, Mr. and Mrs. Grove, and others." [2] These were artists, of course, not millionaires. Eggleston found Grove gruff and brusque, his voice having "a rather harsh, guttural sound, not unpleasant—reminded me of German farmers I used to know just outside of Regina," [3] but they got along well together and "My wife and I were among the warmest friends the Groves made in Ottawa . . . and this friendship persisted over the years." Grove talked freely to him of his dreams: he thought he should be made a member of the diplomatic corps or that he should be made a senator, though he lacked both the urbanity and the ability to compromise of the diplomat, and "his political and economic ideas were naïve." At the end of April, the Egglestons helped the Groves move to a rented summer cottage, which was hard to find and difficult to get to, on the Skead Road near the Ottawa River, where they lived until they left Ottawa in the fall of 1931. During that time, their son Arthur Leonard, named after Phelps, was born on October 14, 1930.

Whatever social disappointments there may have been, the intricate confusion of the Graphic operation would in itself have discouraged a much more patient man than Grove, and by the time Ariston Publishers was incorporated, its president had already threatened to resign. He had discovered that he could not interest United States firms in the Canadian books that he had to offer—apparently he had conceded that it was necessary to have a supporting publisher—he had discovered that he could not legally sign himself president of Ariston since no such officer was designated, and he had come to realize that the firm of Cameron-Solmes ran Graphic in all its operations. In a letter to Mrs. Cameron, dated January 13, 1930, less than six weeks after taking his new job, he said, "I am therefore, strictly speaking, an employee of Cameron Solmes. Would it, then, not be much better if Cameron and Solmes handled all accounts directly and I closed out my [Ariston's] bank account?" Since he was not to have "a determining voice in all affairs of Graphic . . . I cannot give my name; I am content to remain a mere employee, nameless and anonymous, as far as the public is concerned." However, he did outline a plan for the distribution of his work and the $3,600 salary, one-third to be charged to Ariston, one-third to Canadian Biographies, a Graphic project, and one-third to editorial work for Graphic. The plan did not last long, for in April, the day after the official incorporation, he wrote Mrs. Cameron again, demanding more money, "at the least $500 a month, and that from April 1st on"; otherwise, he would quit. Since Grove stayed on for another year and a half, presumably the money was forthcoming.

Two activities undertaken by Graphic may have helped to keep his interest. One was a novel contest, which Grove later claimed to have opposed, but since two of his protégés, Marcus Adeney and Mrs. Wallis of Calgary, won second and third prizes, while the first prize went to Raymond Knister, for whom Grove claimed to have "manoeuvered" it, and since his efforts were in keeping with his announced desire to encourage Canadian writing, it is likely that he was not averse to the contest at the time. The other development was a decision by Graphic's directors to publish "older worthwhile literature concerning Canada," to be called The Canada Series, with Grove as the general editor. It is probable that this idea came from Lawrence Burpee, who was president of Graphic for 1930–31, who had been engaged in this kind of work for a considerable time, and who would know what kind of material was available.

An impressive advisory committee was drawn up for the series, composed of A. G. Doughty, the Dominion archivist, George Wrong, professor emeritus of history at Toronto, and Professor Waugh of history at McGill, and the Graphic catalogue for 1930–31 announced, "Four volumes have been planned for the first year, two to appear in the fall of 1930, the next two in the spring of 1931." Three did appear, but all in 1931. The first was *Dr. Cheadle's Journal of a Trip Across Canada 1862–63*, edited by A. G. Doughty; the next, *The History of Emily Montague*, a novel published in London in 1769, edited by Burpee; and the third was Lahontan's *Voyages*, edited by Stephen Leacock, which appeared in only a few copies and those without Leacock's knowledge. As he later wrote, "I received, through Dr. Burpee of Ottawa, a contract with the Graphic Company to do an introduction to Lahontan's Journal, with notes. . . . The Company failed and paid nothing. . . . But I found out long afterwards that some copies of the book had gone through the press, though it was never on the market. . . . I was never able to get a copy." [4] Since of the three works that did appear in this series, one was edited by Graphic's president, one by Stephen Leacock at his request, and the third by the Dominion archivist who was also a member of the project's committee, Grove's editorship would seem to have been more nominal than most.

Leacock's account also reveals the active part that Burpee was taking as a literary adviser. Grove was not, as he claimed in *In Search of Myself*, the only one at Graphic who knew anything about books. Another person who knew about books in a different way was the production manager, Fred Pain, who had served his apprenticeship at bookmaking in England, where he had won a prize for typography, and who seemed to be the only one who was interested in or knew how to compute production costs. Indeed, Graphic had a number of gifted, enthusiastic, self-sacrificing people all devoted to the furthering of Canadian arts and artists, but each, like Grove, with his own idea of how that should be done. The very fact that they were such idealists, that this was not just an ordinary business venture, but something they felt deeply about accounted for the depth of the bitterness that developed. What the group lacked most was someone experienced in the publishing business. The other great need was money. And money grew scarcer and scarcer as the Great Depression got fully under way. Grove could fulfill neither need, and it is unlikely that he had any effect on Graphic's fortunes for good or ill.

October 1930 was a crowded month for Grove. On October 14, his son was born. In October, *The Yoke of Life* was published. In October there appeared the only two volumes that Ariston did publish and for which Grove was responsible: the first was *The Exquisite Gift*, a new title for Mrs. Wallis's novel, *Here Came a Mortal* that she had submitted to Macmillan; the other one was *The Tide of Life* by Watson Kirkconnell, the second volume of his verse to be published through Graphic. Neither book made a stir.

In October, too, the Louis Carrier Publishing Company went into bankruptcy. Since Miller seems to have done the actual printing, in Ottawa, of Carrier's edition of *A Search for America*, it is probably at this time that Grove got the plates of that edition which Mrs. Grove much later—October 8, 1947—wrote Lorne Pierce about: "The plates contain the type of the whole book and jacket as published by Carrier. They are in small wooden boxes —about 12 of them. My husband paid $300.00 for them." It would be at this time, too, that Grove bought Carrier's unused stock of *The Search*. There were one thousand bound copies that Grove later sent to Dent, who managed to sell about half of them, and there were two thousand sheets, "folded, not gathered, and, of course, unbound," that he sold to Ryerson in December 1938, and that Ryerson issued as their edition in 1939. These sheets were no doubt the consignment that Carrier had sent to Brentano's for the English market, but Brentano's had folded too.

The other thing that was taking up Grove's time was the reading of the manuscripts that were arriving for the Graphic novel contest whose deadline was December 30. Three prizes had been announced: $2,500, $1,500, and $1,000. Three judges had been announced: Barker Fairley of the University of Toronto, W. T. Allison of the University of Manitoba, and Grove (*Canadian Bookman*, April 1930). All prize-winning novels were guaranteed publication "in the fall of 1931."

It was at this time that a friendship began between Grove and

Raymond Knister, Grove twice Knister's age. Their names had been linked a year or so before when Jonathan Cape advertised in England, "Two Canadian Novels"—*Our Daily Bread* and Knister's *The White Narcissus*. Then, too, Knister had reviewed *Our Daily Bread* for *Saturday Night*—" a silly review," Grove had written his wife, "the reviewer has not even read the book." However, when they met briefly in Toronto during Grove's 1929 eastern tour, they got along agreeably, and during Grove's brief associate editorship in *The Canadian Nation* he urged Knister to send in short stories, one of which, "The Fate of Mrs. Lucier," did appear in the final issue. The manuscript that Knister submitted for the Graphic contest, a biographical novel about Keats, *My Star Predominant*, was much longer than the announced maximum, and it is amusing to see Grove as the practical, hard-headed publisher writing to Knister, December 25, 1930, to persuade him to cut it: "I am only one of three judges. But, if you can get the book into manageable form (we cannot consider a novel of more than 100,000 words for a two-dollar book; and we cannot publish, in Canada, at a higher price and make expenses) I can almost promise an offer of publication, prize or no prize, provided, of course, that my present connection with Graphic and Ariston does not come to a smash-up before that consummation." Knister obliged.

There was a small flurry when Allison was found to have chosen three quite different novels from those that Grove and Fairley had agreed upon, but he was overruled, and the prizes were duly announced by March 31: First prize, $2,500, *My Star Predominant* by Raymond Knister; second prize, $1,500, *New Babylon*, a city story of class conflicts in Ontario, by Marcus Adeney; third prize, $1,000, *Happy Issue*, a story of a doctor in a small Ontario town, by Ella B. Wallis. All three were "listed and described in Graphic's final catalogue," but none of them was published by Graphic.[5]

As for Graphic and Grove, relations had become angry and distant. In February he wrote Kirkconnell that he rarely heard anything of the Graphic people though he was still reading manuscripts for them, and just before the prizes were announced in March he broke with the company. He wrote Knister: "the thing is done and I feel free and clean again since I have shaken these commercial shackles; I'd rather teach; perhaps I'd rather starve."

Graphic was approaching disaster, and the fact became general knowledge with the difficulties that arose over the prize money for the contest. Mrs. Wallis got her $1,000 in June; Adeney got $500 of his prize then and the rest later. But as for Knister, he wrote the Canadian Authors' Association from Montreal, "I got my first money the end of August, $300!" [6] Bits of money were now and then paid him, but when Graphic's accounts were placed in the hands of an official trustee in May 1932, the "Statement of Affairs" listed among the debts, "$1000 to Raymond Knister." [7] Graphic Publishers was one of the "Items in Bankruptcy" on August 16, 1932, in the *Toronto Star*. The whole debt of the company, in the trustee's estimate, was only $13,767.97.

It is worth noting that Grove did not appear in the trustee's list of Graphic's creditors, neither in the preferred list of employees to whom wages were due—Fred Pain was among them— nor in the list of authors to whom royalties were due. He seems to have closed out all of his affairs with Graphic before he left Ottawa in October 1931. According to Phelps, the venture "before its collapse, made him a little money. With that money he bought a farm in Western Ontario, with dreams of being a gentleman farmer and literary man. The project was as pathetic as it was ambitious." [8] Grove's career as a publisher was finished. The next dream began as the family arrived at the farm two miles north of Simcoe on October 14, Leonard's first birthday.

PART IV

Man of the Land

CHAPTER 13

The Settler

FROM THE time when Grove saw the southern Ontario countryside on his first tour in the spring of 1928, he was charmed
by it: "I love this country with its cedars and white pines and
apple orchards," he wrote his wife. "Living is cheaper here, too,
than in the West." He was attracted also by the town of Simcoe,
population about five thousand. In the early fall of 1931, he returned to the Simcoe area and bought a forty-acre farm with a
spacious barn, various outbuildings, and a handsome white frame
farmhouse set in a cedar and spruce grove, with a church just
beyond. The purchase price was $7,000, of which he paid $2,000
and covered the rest by a mortgage held by the Agricultural Development Board of Ontario.[1]

The handsome house was badly in need of repair, and he wrote
Knister in Montreal a month later, "we have had to refloor, re-
plaster, repaper, repaint the interior; and we have now lovely
rooms, 10 of them, but there is hardly anything in them: our living room boasts that magnificent Chinese rug which you may
remember and a set of gorgeous old-gold curtains but nothing
else. We spent the afternoon in it, romping with Leonard who
enjoys the spaciousness of it all. And the room is beautiful to me
even without furniture."

Fiction and reality were in a new fusion: the handsome frame
house was another "white range-line house," for it stood on the
corner lot, Lot No. 1, of Concession 12, and Grove was fulfilling
the dream of all his heroes: he had the mansion, the symbol of
achievement. He had become Canadian in that mental and physical sense which he had so often extolled in lectures and novels,
in which people "can stand on soil which they own; for I take it
to be a desire still inherent in man as born by woman to own
that bit of land whence, with tentative mind, he reaches out
into the dark mysteries which surround him." He was also enter-

ing the most desirable of man's estates, the life of the agriculturalist, the free, independent man, a slave to no one, the backbone
of the country, the doer of God's will—a life whose superiority
he had preached and exemplified in all his writing. Within a
matter of weeks he was invited to speak to a neighboring community, where he "delivered a stirring and thought provoking
address on 'The True Farmer.' He displayed a deep understanding of the aspirations of the tiller of the soil and argued con-
vincingly for a well-populated countryside with contented stand-
ards of living." [2] He gave the same address at intervals in the
following year to various groups of the area, always insisting
(perhaps to convince himself as much as his audience), "One can
only live the true life in the open country."

There was the working side of the ideal farmer, of course, and
to that end he bought six purebred Jersey cows, at an average
of $100 a head, for the great, spacious barn, where above each
stall he had the record of the animal's pedigree, its age, its record
in milk and fat production—details impressive enough to be noted
later in the newspaper as of interest to the Norfolk County Jersey
Producers. For the time being, Grove could hire men to do the
farm work, as he had hired them to renovate the house, and for
expert advice there was Munro Landon, president of the County
Chamber of Commerce, a director of the Canadian Jersey Cattle
Club, and also district chairman of the Federation of Ontario
Naturalists, to whom Grove often went about his cows and his
chickens and his crops. Landon said: "Grove was no farmer! He
was a very impractical man. He depended on a man to do his
farm work for him. About all that Grove got out of it was a rural
place to live. You just can't farm that way, it's too expensive, and
Grove didn't have the money." [3]

The rural place to live was probably what Grove prized most
deeply, and with Landon and other naturalists of the county who
were active in a vigorous movement of conservation and protec-
tion of wild life he returned, after the sojourn in the city, to
one of his first loves. Among these congenial men he seems to
have had the warmest companionship that he ever knew: "He
was quiet with us," one of them said.

But the rural life could be prized the more if it could be combined with intellectual interests, with the opportunities that a

town provided. Very shortly there began monthly meetings of the English Club in the Groves' large room. Grove organized the club and planned the programs. At first he also allotted the assignments; on occasion he wrote out fairly detailed outlines of what was to be said, gave several papers himself, and ordered the books, which the members bought from him. Hardy was the subject for the first season, drama the next, and when the club moved out of the Groves' house and into town, D. H. Lawrence was studied one year and Aldous Huxley the following year. For the first two years that the Groves were at Simcoe, there were also Carnegie Foundation lectures on art and literature, organized by McMaster University, for which Grove was chairman the first year—Arthur Lismer gave a series on Renaissance painting— and from which he got a small income the second year as one of the lecturers. For his series of five lectures on "How to Appreciate Literature" he drew largely on his previous papers, on *It Needs to Be Said,* and on books sent him from London City Library by its librarian, Richard Crouch, who, like Kirkconnell in Manitoba, kept up a shuttle service of books for Grove's interest and use. Then too, for the first two or three years, Grove was in demand throughout the district to give talks on literature, education, and New Canadians.

Other gatherings came occasionally to the Groves' large room. The Manitoban Woodsworth, who had known Grove for some years and who with his colleagues had entertained him in Ottawa, became the head of a new political party, the Co-operative Commonwealth Federation (CCF), and organizational meetings were held in Simcoe, as they were in many communities. Although Grove had no formal relationship with the new party so far, when Woodsworth visited Simcoe he stayed with Grove, who invited townspeople out to meet him. The association led Grove into one of his curious hassles.

Among the people who were interested in the new party was Simcoe's mayor, Percy Carter, who, in the spring of 1935 invited the mayor of Toronto, James Simpson, apparently also interested in the CCF, to address a meeting in the town. He asked Grove to chair the meeting. To everyone's astonishment, when Mayor Simpson began to speak, Grove arose and stalked out. He wrote a letter to the editor, dated April 20:

Why, so it has been asked, did I consent to preside over the meeting . . . and why, moreover, having consented, did I leave when Mayor Simpson began to speak?

Briefly, Mr. Carter had appealed to me because, according to him, only someone like myself, standing outside of politics, could lend dignity to the proposed meeting. He asked me to introduce the speaker and to be one of the speakers myself. . . . The point is that, unless I was given the chance to speak ever so briefly—and naturally I planned to do so while introducing the chief speaker—my presence in the chair was indeed incongruous.

Had Mr. Carter asked me in the first place to act as a vaudeville announcer and then to introduce him, it goes without saying that I should have politely but firmly declined. Yet that is exactly the part profoundly distasteful to me, which Mr. Carter and his associates manoeuvred me into playing. The moment I realized this, I had no choice but to leave at once. I left the chair and the meeting when I convinced myself that these gentlemen had no intention of keeping faith with me.

Simcoe's mayor, as baffled as the rest of the audience must have been, also had a letter in the same issue, "to correct an impression that is being circulated to the effect that I brought Mr. James Simpson, Mayor of Toronto, to Simcoe to speak for and on behalf of the C.C.F. and thus trick some people. Nothing was further from my thoughts. . . . If anything happened that was not proper or anyone's feelings were hurt, I am very sorry and wish to apologize for same. I wish to state that I am not associated with any political party." As Mr. Birkinshaw of Rapid City said, Grove was a very easy man to quarrel with—or differ with.

The main purpose of the large room and the spacious house and grounds—a very practical one—appeared shortly after the busy renovations of the Groves' first month in Simcoe. It was the opening of the Froebel Kindergarten; most of the pupils were children of members of the English Club. With this development, Grove returned to his first vocation and to those concepts most deeply ingrained in him, the concepts of nineteenth-century educational philosophy that he stressed in the two 1914 articles: the aim of education as the perception of unity in all things, the path to that perception being away from books to practical learning through workshop, farm, and garden, with specific emphasis on mathematics and nature study, which would lead the child through those stages which were the microview of the cultural epochs of the human race. Conveniently adjoining the Grove farm was a wild-life woodlot set aside by the municipality as part of their conservation plan, which became one of the chief classrooms for the children of this school which was named for the man who had coined the word "kindergarten" to describe the "symbolically important play which is the child's natural activity." Leonard Grove recalled that when he was old enough to join in, "it was all a very pleasant, idyllic sort of time for me. I'd get up in the morning, and the car would bring a whole bunch of kids to play, you know—really what it amounted to. Also there was a certain amount of school work involved but, being an only child and having nobody around constantly, I was quite prepared for the condition that if all these kids were going to come and play with you, then you were going to have to play by sitting at a desk part of the time. Other people have told me about their troubles going to public school. I don't remember that at all. It all seemed like a holiday to me." [4]

Before the second year began, Grove advertised the prospectus of the Froebel Kindergarten School in the Simcoe paper, July 7, 1932. Fees, payable in advance monthly, were $5 a month for a half day of instruction, $10 a month for a full day of instruction; the studies would be "more or less along the lines of the Ontario Programme of Studies for Kindergarten-Primary schools"; and "the school is further expanding its work and will be prepared to take any Public School form for full day instruction. With the beginning of the first form, age 6 or 7, oral French, nature study, home geography and art will be taught in addition to the subjects prescribed. . . . The school is conducted by Mrs. F. P. Grove with Mr. F. P. Grove and Miss A. Wiens assisting." Amanda Wiens was Mrs. Grove's youngest sister, in her early twenties, who had recently received her teacher's certificate in Saskatchewan.

The school grew for a time, so that in 1935 another classroom was added to accommodate ten more pupils, for whom "a bus service will take care of transportation," the notice in the *Reformer* said, and income from the school for the 1934–35 session was $2,000.

CHAPTER 14

The Literary Man

ABOVE THE large room, to the left at the top of the stairs, was the gentleman-farmer, the man of letters, the master of all this in a small westward-looking study that was half-filled with an enormous desk, its right-hand top drawer full of sharp-pointed pencils. The master himself was "tall, very spare, always beautifully dressed. He dressed almost in the English squire clothes— the heavy tweeds, the heavy brown brogues. He was a very imposing man." [1] His literary stature was also noted when, after *Fruits of the Earth* was at last published, Grove received the Lorne Pierce Gold Medal for literary merit from the Royal Society of Canada, an award that was proudly announced by the *Reformer*, March 1, 1934, for "he is the only Ontario citizen in the list of awards made this year by the Royal Society." He had been recognized earlier, in April 1932, by *The Canadian Forum* as a subject for an article in their series, "Canadian Writers of Today," and in the same issue the *Forum* published three pages of his verse, the largest amount of Grove's verse ever published. The article, however, turned out to be a left-handed compliment, for Robert Ayre, who wrote it, was not laudatory. [2] The article so rankled with Grove that he enshrined this critic in the "Ant Book."

And it was to the "Ant Book" that Grove now returned. Three hard-cover scribblers, filled with his careful handwriting and dated October 1933, contain the sweeping revision of "MAN, His Habits, Social Organisation, and Outlook." The pulpit thumping is gone. Only the introduction survives from the script of eight years before. This is a new work, new in conception, in tone, and in the quality of the prose. It is a lively narrative of another of Grove's far-travelers. It was this text which was used some fourteen years later, with a few minor changes, for *Consider Her Ways*. [3]

It is easy to see the new "Ant Book" evolving from the success of *A Search for America.* Both books are intended as critiques of society, but whereas Phil Branden said, "I had to restrict my view of it to the view from below, to the perspective of the frog," the new search for America is undertaken by the lower animal world in the scholar-ant, Wawa-quee and her retinue. It is a view from below, not only because of the minuteness of the viewer, but also because she comes from down under, from the South. For the circumstantial details of her travels, Grove used Bates, *A Naturalist on the River Amazon,* for the South American part; Thomas Belt, *A Naturalist in Nicaragua;* Father Sumichrast un "Mexican Hymenoptera"[4] for the isthmus; and from there on, Wheeler's fascinating ant book, which Grove adapted with great freedom, using Wheeler's sociological reflections, describing localities that were in fact photographs in Wheeler's volume, and using Wheeler himself as a character—"the wheeler"—who crops up once in a while in Wawa-quee's sojourn. As Branden came from another region and another civilization to take "a cross-section of a continent," to view the New World with candid eyes, so Wawa-quee comes from another region and another civilization, but her task is greater; she views the whole race of man.

Part of the unusual quality of the book, part of its attraction is that neither of these worlds, the ant world nor the human world, is an imaginary world, as those were that Gulliver, Christian, or Ralph Hythloday visited. Both of them are real, factual. The journey is into a known world of man, and however astonishing the life and habits of the various ant races, they too belong to the realm of fact, not fiction. This double vision, or "compound picture," as Grove called it, gives added texture to the shifts from the ant world to the non-ant world in the triangular journey from the Orinoco up to the Colorado Mountains, across the plain to New York, and thence back again. Yet as the *Times Literary Supplement* reviewer said of Ferenczy's ant book, we become so interested in the ants as ants that we lose any vivid awareness of critical comparisons with human beings. The book is ineffective as satire, but it is distinctive in another way, as Grove noted in a letter to Pierce, March 25, 1940, when he said, "Perhaps there is as much laughter in it as I shall ever evoke."

The overall view of the female-dominated ant society is, of course, of great relevance to Grove's continuing theme of changing biological organization in the human race. Their queen, like the poet of "The Canyon," is fertilized only once; they are capable of parthenogenesis, a feat that is intimated of Jane Atkinson; and the narrator is bisexual, or perhaps omnisexual.

An expedition of Atta Gigantea ants is sent north by the reigning queen of "the great and glorious formicary in the valley of the Orinoco River" for the purpose of completing a survey of antdom so that a definitive catalogue of classifications may be drawn up. The expedition under the leadership of Wawa-quee starts out with five groups of scientists numbering 162 altogether —geographers, botanists, zoologists, communications experts, and recorders—accompanied by a protecting army of 10,000 under a separate commander. They travel up the isthmus by night marches through the land of their deadly enemies, the warrior Ecitons; in the mountains they find the pastoral, aphid-milking ants and, when they reach the Garden of the Gods in Colorado in their fifth summer, they see the honey ants with their living storehouses, the repletes. On leaving the mountains, they meet the harvesting ants on the eastern slope, the slave-makers on the plains, and eventually they come to a man-dominated, almost antless world in the city on the seaboard, where the learned ants walking up and down the books in the New York Public Library absorb the contents through their own techniques.

Disasters of many kinds befall them, from nature, from other ants, from men as Wheeler scoops up a portion of the army, and from within themselves. A barnyard hen demolishes twenty scientists; red ants massacre the army; an automobile roars by and "Sixty-six great scholars . . . were reduced to a greasy smear on a highway"; crossing the Mississippi, five hundred soldiers are killed by lightning; the army commander and her surviving followers are executed for treason. Of the whole expedition, only three scholars reach the seaboard, and only one returns to the valley of the Orinoco.

A few strokes outline characters. Anna-zee, the chief botanist, is a skeptic, "in her slow and sardonic way . . . nodding her head sideways over her left shoulder." She is one of those smeared on the highway. The zoologist, Bissa-tee, on the other hand, is a big, breezy, thorax-thumping, but nonetheless intelligent companion. Assa-ree, the army commander, is sinister from the beginning, with her strange odor and her ill-concealed insolence. It is the growth and gradual revelation of her treachery that give shape and suspense to the story line. Then there is Wawa-quee, the leader of the expedition, the author's "I." In the earlier version, Grove made no attempt to present a convincing or even a masking fictional figure. But as Wawa-quee says, "Let me skip an interval of eight years and speak of the present." Wawa-quee is still Grove, but there is now an amusing distancing. She points out that she is old, much older than one should be to conduct such an expedition; that she can be distinguished in a crowd by her huge head, rather than by any handsome physical attributes; and that the huge head is a sign of her valuable brain. She has an innocent vanity, a pleasure in her abilities. Invited to give a lecture on her experiences, she says, "If I do say it myself, though my own interests are exclusively scientific, I seem to have the gift of carrying away the masses." She recounts the infatuation of two queens for her and admits that she is not above resentment and retaliation, the most notable example being when she sinks her mandibles into the soft thigh flesh of a young woman in the Public Library. She can be ruthless. When Bissa-tee questions her about the justice of her summary execution of the army, she says quite coolly, "it was she or we, that is all. . . . Justice is not a question of right but of might." She can indulge in self-pity: "I saw myself, or rather the three of us, struggling again through snow and sleet and rain, the human road roaring with noise and traffic; and I felt sorry for myself." It is the admission that is significant.

There is little doubt that, on a level different from that of the trite symbolism of the mountains and of the slave-makers of the plains, Grove was drawing a loose analogy with his own life leading up to and away from Ottawa, beginning with the lecture tour, the isthmus, when he wrote his wife of his "gift of carrying away the masses." It was in Ottawa, "the Garden of the Gods," that he met the repletes, the honey storers, the writers "suspended above the common herd," "hanging from the roof of their circumscribed world," "debarred from all friendly and intimate intercourse," "ostentatiously honoured and secretly despised as unnecessary and unproductive members of society" (112–17)— phrases that he was obviously applying to himself also. Attendant upon the writers are others called critics. Leaving the Garden, it was "much harder to descend the mountains than to ascend them. Not a day went by without casualties" (119). And there is the episode with the man Ayr, who tried to "crush me out of existence," and so "I want to hand at least his appelation over to the everlasting condemnation of antkind" (246). Then there is a quite astonishing passage within the last fifteen pages of the book. It is probably the most intimate scene in all of Grove's writing, sensitive, compassionate, and self-critical. It is the account of the growing estrangement between the two survivors of the great struggle, Bissa-tee and Wawa-quee, as they reach a point on the return journey where they had been six years before:

A whole compound organism had been functioning; and we had been part of that organism. It had carried us along. Now that organism had disappeared; the task, apart from reporting our results, had been accomplished or abandoned. . . . I had more than once reflected upon the desirability, if not the absolute necessity, of observing the strictest forms of politeness all the more punctiliously when any discourtesy on my part was apt to be interpreted as pointing directly against the only companion I had left. . . . But, instead of feeling compunction on account of my rudeness, I resented the interpretation she put upon my silence. . . . We did not even wish each other good night. . . . Every now and then I caught Bissa-tee, now recovered to a point to which I, being so much older, could not recover any longer, looking wistfully across the brook and scanning the horizon; and I knew that she was blaming me in her heart . . . when my anger had reached an explosive pressure, I emitted a faint scent of rally. I did this only to relieve myself; I never thought it would reach Bissa-tee. But it did, and she veered around, snarling. I will throw a scent-screen over the scene that followed. For more than an hour we indulged in mutual recriminations. Both of us were partly in the right; and that fact blinded us to that other fact that we were both wholly in the wrong. . . . I retired to our temporary quarters, angry and despondent, but at the same time longing for comfort and companionship, longing for Bissa-tee to come and make it up. She did at last; slowly and shame-facedly she came in. . . . Both of us felt stirred to our depths; and we begged forgiveness from each other, blaming fate, blaming the state we were in; feeling sorry for each other, feeling sorry for our-selves. (282-86)

There are recurrent references to six years earlier in the fifteen pages, which bring the matter of dates forcibly to mind. This manuscript is dated October 1933. Six years before was shortly after the death of May. In those six years, after grief, had come the high hopes and the bitter disappointments of the Ottawa venture.

This section stands out the more because it is not characteristic of the general tone of the book. That tone is in the permeating but inoffensive assumption of the superiority of the Atta race; it is in the incongruity of great wisdom and minute form; it is in blunt statement as when the recording scholar was "crushed to a pulp"; it is in Wawa-quee's conclusions that are based on man's books, "not on what man consciously meant to put down, but on a critical interpretation of what he put into them without being aware of its import." Much of the sense of perspective and the easy quality of the prose comes from the character of the ant-narrator. It would seem that Grove was no longer talking to his pupils but that he was at ease among his peers.

The level of writing in the revision of the "Ant Book," unfortunately, was not sustained. Once again Grove set about writing his farm novel, placing his themes and theories against the setting in which he currently lived, as he had done before. The result he called *Two Generations,* and he wrote Lorne Pierce, on November 21, 1938, saying: "It is the first of my 'pleasant' books which I offer; and it is the first Ontario novel which I have written, the date of composition being 1931/36. It even has a 'happy ending.'"

The dating is characteristic of Grove, for he commonly took as part of the writing time—or of the creative process—the time of his first acquaintance with the area which he used for the setting. In the same way, he dated *Settlers* 1917-24. This method of dating, of course, made the period between writing and publishing seem very long indeed, though the time between completing a manuscript and its publication may not have been remarkable.

Two Generations is the story of two years, 1928-29, in the life of a family who own two farms in the neighborhood of Simcoe, one on the outskirts of town, the other some fifteen miles away, the mother's inheritance. Ralph Patterson, a household tyrant with touches from Soames Forsyte, tries to keep his children on his farm as underpaid help. They rebel. Ungraciously acknowledging fact, he gives one parcel of land to a son who wants to be a florist, grudgingly agrees to the marriage of another with a ballet dancer, but quarrels so bitterly with a third son who wants to go to university to become an astronomer that the son leaves home and with him goes the eldest daughter who enters medical college at Toronto. Between these two there is a love stronger than that usually between brother and sister (shades of the Forsytes again), but they help each other "in the face of a tragic experience." Their mother gives them part of her farm to help them through university, but she reserves another part for herself and her husband. Very wisely, because in the stock market crash of 1929, he is ruined. Humbled, he does the most courageous thing of his life. He apologizes to his son for all his harshness, and everyone is happy thereafter. It is all rather dull. It is also the kind of novel in which a man going to the woodshed and filling the washtub for a bath, "performed his ablutions."

As for this being an Ontario novel, it is as much an Ontario novel as Grove's earlier novels were Manitoba novels. Both have descriptions of particular trees and flowers; both have blizzards; and both have analyses of snow formations. In *Fruits of the Earth,* people braving a blizzard arrive at the farmhouse for Christmas dinner: in *Two Generations,* people braving a blizzard arrive at a farmhouse on Christmas Eve. In *Fruits of the Earth,* there is detailed technical description of the harness of horses pulling a culvert into place; in *Two Generations,* there is detailed description of the working of a milking machine. Patterson is a younger John Elliot; he is Abe Spalding's double, and like Niels Lindstedt, he is said to be a pioneer, though the appellation sits a little awkwardly on this farmer in well-settled Ontario. Yet, "he belonged to that class which, tragically, strives after an end that defeats itself. The pioneer wants to fight the wilderness back: and as he fights it back, he changes it into what is no longer wilderness; and then he moves on" (255). John Steinbeck wrote of the spirit of westering sensitively and well; but those driven by westering or pioneering were not dairy farmers on inherited land in Ontario. As he did so often, Grove here was trying to lift a commonplace, humdrum story into the heroic or the tragic simply by misapplying words.

The title announces the book's affinity with *Our Daily Bread* in its theme of the conflict of generations, the theme which had already had its trilogy run and had then reappeared in *Fruits of the Earth,* which, after all, had won a Royal Society award. In fact, *Two Generations* is the second half of *Fruits of the Earth* including the happy ending; the variations are peripheral. There is the great handsome house now emptying, the man who "has worked like a slave; he has worked like a Titan," who finds his children leaving the parental home, who is bewildered to discover that they have minds of their own, to discover the mystery of a child's individuality. Yet he is so much of the individual himself that he is blind and brutal toward others as he exemplifies once more Grove's "I am what I am," the "abiding substratum" which is not subject to change but which constitutes the laws of the individual identity. The modification here is that he does apologize. There is honor to the agricultural life, the usual remarks about the central role of the farmer and the parasitic one of the city dweller, but there is also the concession, as in *Our Daily Bread,* that university education can be a good thing. Another modification is in the character of Nancy, the ballet dancer. For once in Grove's novels, dancing is not a symbol of sin. Indeed, Nancy is a muted Clara Vogel; she is unfaithful to her husband both before and after marriage. This is a great departure from earlier insistence on "purity." Now love conquers all. She loves her husband while she is sleeping with other men; he, though horrified, loves her too. Part of the tolerance lies in the fact that she is a gifted artist and one earning a very good living of her own. But she, like Len of the *Yoke,* "had spiritually sailed the seven seas" (165).

One point of some interest in this novel is that Grove identifies both with the autocratic father of "savage humour," and with his rebellious son called Phil. The double identification accounts for the fluctuating age of Ralph Patterson—a similar fluctuation occurred in *A Search for America*—who at forty-five is in the prime of his vigorous life, but his purpose in living has come to an end; he feels empty, useless. This man who owns two farms and a dairy herd is at a loss as to how to use his time, and he waits impatiently for the train to come in so that he can drive to town for the mail and have something to do. In common with many of Grove's men, he begins a new life in his forties, but at the same time he is figured as the old Ulysses, the idle king with an aged wife—the emotional reality of his creator now nearing sixty. But that creator was also identifying himself with the young son of twenty who clashed with his father because, his mother tells him, "you are so exactly alike."

When to this oneness is added the further oneness between Phil and his sister, things begin to get a bit murky on the literal level. The sister has a melodramatic bent too: "Phil and I are Ishmaels . . . orphans of the soul . . . We should have been twins" (185). With this involved identity or multiple oneness there comes again the hermaphroditic figure, the symbol of the primordial creator. Yet while these aspects of the novel are worth noting in their general relation to Grove's other work, *Two Generations* remains the weakest of all his novels on agricultural life.

At about the same time, Grove was working out the generations theme in yet another context. *The Master of the Mill* was to be the ultimate Canadian novel. It embraced everything. Set in 1938, the time of Grove's writing, the story recedes, through flashbacks in the mind of the present mill owner, Senator Sam Clark, to the first Clark who started a mill and who died in 1867, the year Canada came into existence. Geographically, the mill is located in the middle of the country, near the western Ontario border around Kenora; but with four branches in the west and a satellite mill in the east, it spans the nation. It is the hub of the nation economically and politically, for "wheat being its principal produce, control of the mill, in the long run, means control of the country" (219). Its operations involve laborers, managers, scientists, politicians, and financiers; and its wealth reaches out to gather in the arts. It is the basis of human life, for it provides "our daily bread," and in thus fulfilling a fundamental human need, it has high moral value.

The surface story of the pyramid-shaped mill is that of the little people who built it, the Clark men and their assistants, who "had been mere pygmy helpers in bringing it to life" (328); and repeatedly it is noted that "all directly concerned with the mill were small and spare," with the suggestion that there was possibly "some principle of selection at work" (141). There are three generations of Clarks in the story: Sam, his father Rudyard, and his son Edmund. The usual two divisions in a Grove novel are here: "Death of the Master," and "Resurrection of the Master." The first part is the founding of the present mill and its development under Rudyard; the second is its mechanization and growth as a political power under Edmund, the reincarnation of the ruthless grandfather—"Like my grandfather, I am a tool of destiny; and I was born to wield power" (226). For Sam, the hinge between the two, the dreamer, the designer, the humanitarian, despised and driven from power by both father and son, the title of "Master" is a mockery.

Rudyard, ambitious and unscrupulous, burned down the old mill, built the new one with the money he got from defrauding the insurance company, expanded it into a huge industrial enterprise, within the mill town created interlocking holding companies so that all of the public works as well as the workers' housing were under his control, and exploited the workers as harshly as he did his son. After his death, Sam, who had dreamed of raising wages and giving the workers a voice in governing the mill, discovered the fraud and discovered further that his father had been paying blackmail to a part-time bookkeeper, Bill Swann, who knew of it. He was able to bribe Swann, who returned to his native England, and Sam then devoted all of his energies to preserving the mill and his son's inheritance by buying shares and consolidating the management of the mill so that no one would be in a position to inquire into its affairs. The result was that "His father's crime made him, the son, the slave of the mill" (94), and he became as remote and secretive with his son as Rudyard had been with him. But while Edmund was recuperating from war wounds in an English hospital, Swann went to him and told him the whole story. Despising his father's scruples, Edmund ousted Sam from control of the mill, and, following his buccaneering grandfather, he manipulated politicians and financiers, acquired a national monopoly, brought about complete automation of the mill, and goaded the men into striking so that he would appear justified both in the automation and in dismissing superfluous workers. In the course of the strike, he was shot and killed. The strike subsided; the workers lost; the mechanized mill went on. In January 1925, Sam, at seventy, became "Master" of the mill by default.

For the following thirteen years, as the mill ran itself except for the ministrations of a handful of technicians, Sam lived in the great Clark mansion together with two women, Odette Charlebois, companion to his dead wife Maud, and his son's widow Maud who, at his death, would become the next "master," for the line of Clarks had run out. As he nears death, Sam concludes that all three Clarks, not just himself, had been slaves to the mill, their lives sacrificed to a great evolutionary process of freeing men from labor and providing them with food:

Man was born, suffered, and died; but the mill watched over him: this mill and others. The mill was a god to him, all-good, all-provident, all-powerful. It even provided for its own procreation: that mill which was composite of all mills; for its essence was hermaphroditic. (328)

The hermaphroditic deity, served by a priesthood of devoted engineers, chemists, and sweepers, was the culminating revelation of a beneficent nature that exuded from the earth, for "the mill was not a man-made thing: it was an outgrowth of the soil, the rock, the earth, subject to laws of growth of its own" (60), and was made manifest in pyramidal, anthill form by the impulse of its necessary logic working through human activity. The last great step of this beneficent consciousness is the freeing of man from Adam's curse—"In the sweat of thy face shalt thou eat bread"—to lead him to the grand fulfillment of his highest powers as the pinnacle of created beings. It is the cosmic evolutionary plan reaching its consummation after eons of geologic time. It is this force that is the Master of the Mill.

In the vastness of such a movement, the individual Clarks, like the individual workmen, are unimportant, indistinguishable—in effect, one man—just as their women are all one woman, named Maud. In this context, the flashback technique that Grove used gains special significance, both in the mind of the old man for whom time past is indeed time present, and in the evolutionary process in which his life of over eighty years is less than a moment. So, too, the title of the second part, "Resurrection of the Master," gains further significance, for this resurrection is also the Second Coming of the primordial creator.

Within the great encompassing movement of which only a few are even vaguely aware, however, smaller developments take place in human time, the main development being the ongoing action of the industrial revolution bringing the Machine Age. In this action the Clarks are representative stages—Rudyard the laissez-faire freebooter that Carlyle inveighed against; Sam the Victorian liberal, the humanitarian; and Edmund the twentieth-century organizing man, the dictator who, scorning elected government, seeks to become ruler of the "state within a state," the industrial colossus for whom the mill would form "the kernel of a political and economic dictatorship" (246). Edmund claims to be a benevolent despot, quickening the process toward the complete welfare state that his father and his humanitarian contemporaries began, by driving forward to total automation and so lessening the period of suffering, for only when total unemployment is reached can this central problem be dealt with intelligently: "Unemployment is the natural state of man. Unemployment was man's condition in Paradise" (330). In this fashion, the evolutionary process is related to the immediate question of great human distress.

It was not enough, however, for *The Master of the Mill* to comprehend all of Canadian life, and beyond that the general theme of changing cultural epochs, and beyond that the prophetic history of man. These concerns were all terrestrial. In order to reach the furthest limits of Grove's vision, they had to be fitted within the revolving universe. In an appendage of about two and a half pages, this final movement is forecast during an all-night vigil after Sam's funeral by the three black-clad Mauds: Edmund's mother and Sam's wife, present by proxy; Edmund's mistress, who was Sam's early inspiration; and Edmund's wife, the new Master. It is the second of these, the Maud of "heart and instinct" (41), who prophesies that the paradise of unemployment, once reached, will prove ephemeral, the mill will decay, the human race will dwindle, until, many ages in the future, man will again become a hunter and then will "slowly reinvent hammer, lever, and wheel" and once more bring about the industrial revolution. The cycling movement is, of course, at variance with the evolutionary theory which had been the carefully constructed framework of the whole novel. The anomaly does not end there. As in *The Yoke of Life*, so in *The Master of the Mill*, the high-minded discourse comes crashing down in the flatness of its concluding sentence: "I have come to place a great confidence in the capacity of the collective human mind" (332). It is hard to tell who will win, the hermaphroditic deity, the *primum mobile*, or the human race, but Grove was covering all bets.

Apart from "huge, cloudy symbols of a high romance," the great visions of nineteenth-century biological theory which fascinated Grove, there is another layer to this novel, a layer on which Sam is a senator, Edmund is knighted, their wives are aristocrats, there are two mansions filled with footmen, butlers, and maids, and to their gatherings come the high and the mighty. Just as the mill is placed in a particular physical setting, so this layer of the novel is placed in a literary landscape made up of Mann's *Buddenbrooks*, Wells's *The Shape of Things to Come*, and Huxley's *Point Counterpoint*.

It sits there uneasily. The attempt to portray society life, instead of creating an effect of power and elegance and sophistication, sounds merely vulgar. As Macmillan said when writing Grove about "the overdoing of 'footmen' and 'butlers.' . . . It is unnatural and a little like the atmosphere of grandeur-in-a-dream which pervades the literature popular among these gentry themselves. Few of the homes of wealth in Canada were as over-run with flunkeys at any time as this picture would suggest." [5] Like Huxley, Grove presents recognizable public figures in some of his characters, for instance, Arthur Meighen and J. S. Woodsworth; and the character of Edmund owes a good deal to Huxley's Everard Webley, né Moseley; but the attempt to produce a scene like that in Huxley's Tantamount House is a fiasco. The ball at Edmund's mansion in the Ontario countryside begins to "the giddy strains of a waltz by Strauss"; the guests at dinner never sit at tables, but only at "boards"; and they conduct incredible conversations. And in everyday life, two women alone just before lunch, "being both at leisure, and Odette, betraying the desire to continue their conversation, they sat down" (70). The language is constantly betraying the attempt at refinement.

Like H. G. Wells, Grove was fascinated with machinery, whether threshing machine, milking machine, or mill machine, and, as in other of his novels, some of the most effective and genuinely interesting passages are those describing machines and the details of their working. But whereas in earlier novels Grove viewed with alarm the coming of the machine age as being a deterioration from the agricultural epoch, in *The Master of the Mill* he has changed, and, following Wells, he sees the machine as man's ultimate benefactor, doing away with exploitation and poverty. Moreover, his utopia, like Wells's, is not on an isolated, rock-bound island, but within the possibility of everyday life. The ideal that he creates, however, is that of "a state within a state" of disenfranchised, passive beneficiaries.

Within the still more restricted area of the personal lives of his Ontario Buddenbrooks, many of Grove's customary characters and themes appear. The usual questions of the nature of slavery and the nature of the individual permeate the novel, not only in the family, but in the mill, in the workers, in the demands of the machine, and so forth. There is the master-father, slave-son conflict of *Two Generations*, and Sam is another Phil; but as Sam perpetuates the generation conflict, his daughter Ruth is again Phil's rebel sister, but even more she is a reincarnation of Jane Atkinson, for "she was without sex" (204); she could not face "that daily intimacy that marriage implies," and so she married an ancient French marquis of ancient family: "What she married was not a man. It was immunity" (204). Carnality is back again, this time in the person of Sam's sister-in-law Sylvia who is St. Anthony's Queen of Sheba in the mill town. Frigidity or lust—there is no middle way with Grove's people. Neither is there any hint that his dualism would disappear in the paradise of the unemployed.

The second part of the novel is sprawling and formless as the flashback technique gets out of hand, and there is much unrevealing repetition of what happened from Sam, from each of the two women, and from a partially written history of the mill. There is endless reporting of people and events, in which the work does not rise to the level of created fiction, but remains a voluminous notebook, out of which a novel could be formed. Once more, a grandly conceived plan failed in the execution. When Grove completed the manuscript, he wrote to Richard Crouch, on August 17, 1939, "The 'Master' is finished, thank the Lord."

But his mind had already been busy with another ambitious scheme from the spring of 1938, when he wrote Dr. Alexander that he was working on another Ontario novel which for the moment he called "Democracy," which was to present "the whole countryside, town, villages and rural districts in one broad canvas." A couple of years later he wrote Pierce that Part I of this panoramic novel, now called "The Seasons," would cover also the economic, political, and university life of Ontario, that it "might well rank among the great works of the age," and when completed "it will be a book of 1000 printed pages." This project he never did finish, though a manuscript of over 450 pages exists, in quality going back to the 1925 "Ant Book," a ponderous expounding of commonplaces.

He did complete two minor works. One, "Felix Powell's Career," he sent to Pierce, saying that it was "a college story with a multiple sexual theme," possibly influenced by the English Club's study of Lawrence. The initials F—— P—— seem to suggest that Grove was once more drawing attention to himself.[6] Pierce returned it May 6, 1940, saying it was "one of the most readable manuscripts you have done. . . . Your picture of Felix Powell is a champion portrait of a cad. He is a very common type, and might need a book written on him," but Ryerson was obviously not interested in publishing it. The manuscript is said to have been destroyed later by Mrs. Grove. The other was a novelette, *The Adventure of Leonard Broadus*, "a juvenile" Grove called it, "crammed with action," about the 1939 visit of King George VI to Canada. Lorne Pierce managed to sell that for him to *The Canadian Boy*, a paper distributed in United Church Sunday schools, in which the story appeared serially from April to June 1940.

And then there was *In Search of Myself*.[7] On September 3, 1938, he wrote Richard Crouch that he had "suddenly been seized with the inspiration of working up and consolidating the sequel of A Search For America. . . . All day long I write; at night I read what I have written." At the end of November he told Pierce that he was working on a volume tentatively entitled "In Search of Myself," dealing with the twenty-six years following *America;* but it was not until March 1940 that he sent him a completed manuscript. Writing Grove about it, Pierce said that while it was "splendid commentary upon your own life's work," he had hoped that it would also mention "some interesting contemporary men and movements, especially in the arts and letters. There were important things being done in both fields, and out of this milieu your own work came. Looking back it strikes me that you lived through a time that saw the actual birth of a native arts and letters."

Not only the world of arts and letters and of national movements is lacking; the book as a whole is disappointingly empty. It does not stand by itself as having its own validity of interest, as *A Search for America* does. What interest it has accrues from a reader's previous interest in Grove's other writing. Even then it is thin and unrewarding.

Less than half of the 457 pages do, in fact, deal with the twenty-six years following upon *A Search for America.* The first two sections and a considerable part of the third are simply elaborations on the story of *America,* but without its effectiveness. The Walter Mitty European background has grown luxuriantly. A flash of a prostitute in a lighted doorway, the echoing song of Kirghiz herdsmen on the Russian Steppes, a warehouse in Java that Lord Jim might have mistaken for Stein's, elegance in Vienna, gourmet living in Paris, a succession of universities, seduction by the older woman, a beautiful, impetuous mother who died of a lingering illness, the spendthrift father wasting his son's substance, as he did in *America,* but now dashing, sadistic, and eventually so crippled by disease that he became a hunchback. The adventures of the immigrant, too, have been multiplied to extend over twenty years rather than the two years of *America,* and they are correspondingly thinner, more vague. There is an attempt to fill in these years with five unbelievable return journeys to the unbelievable Europe.

In the section that does deal with the period following the *America* story, "MY LIFE AS A WRITER IN CANADA," which was the first title of the book, and which remains as the last phrase, in capitals, of the prologue, a reader expects some depth of concern with literary affairs, some insight into Grove's thought processes, but there is very little material of that sort. In fact, this part of the book is not much more than an annotated ledger. The concern for money, which Grove constantly deprecated in his public utterances and which he continued to deprecate even in these pages, overrides all other interests. He complains frequently of an impoverishment which records do not bear out. On the other hand, he is quite candid about the Graphic venture. When the Groves moved east from Rapid City, they had $5,000 (398); when they left Ottawa they had $7,000 and a mortgage of $1,000 on Graphic property which, he says, they collected. Grove was the only person associated with Graphic to make money out of it, and during the depression a nest egg of $8,000 was, for most people, quite a handsome sum. But the tendency to cry poor was not a new one; it was in *Over Prairie Trails* too.

There is one phrase that sums up Grove's attitude to the entire outside world: "what happened to us . . . *was done by* the east" (409) (my italics). He considered himself the victim, not just of callous indifference, but of active malice. This strong strain of self-pity and self-righteousness is at times breathtaking in view of the world at the time he was writing and the people among whom he was living, who were in the midst of a second world war following a brutal Depression. As Pierce suggested, Grove had a vast unawareness of the rest of the world. There are remarkably few people in his record.

But as with Rousseau's *Confessions,* the outside world or factual truth is of relevance only as it shows how experience was shaped by the writer; beyond that, it is irrelevant. The record that Grove fashions has its own validity, its own truth; this is the life that he lived, the inner landscape that he saw. In his years as a writer, he sees himself as both the elected artist who scorned the multitude and the man whom their indifference has injured. The world that lived in his memory was a world of grudging concessions, of injustices done a worthy person, of bitter tricks of fate. It held neither humor nor warmth nor tolerance nor generosity of mind. Grove's ending—"For everything we acquire so-and-so-much life has to be paid" (452)—goes back to the beginning of his writings and to Thoreau's theory of cost and economy. The basic symbol is the ledger.

In spite of all the writing, except for a handful of short stories and articles, Grove published nothing for nearly six years, from 1933 to 1939. He himself was responsible for at least part of the awkward situation that he was in—altogether aside from the impractical plunge into farming—because of his habit of quarreling with publishers. He wrote to Crouch on October 24, 1938, about finding a publisher for *Two Generations,* saying that he was "reluctant to offer this to Macmillans . . . or to the Ryerson Press or McClelland & Stewart (put it down to personal prejudice). Do you think Reg Saunders might be interested?" Grove did not mention Dent, his latest and one-shot-only publisher, nor of course, the two defunct firms that he also got into difficulties with. His publishing possibilities were limited; and apparently Saunders was not interested.

But with persistence and a good deal of courage, Grove began a plan for publishing *Two Generations* by private subscription in a limited author's edition. Naturally, one of the letters asking for a subscription went to Ryerson. Lorne Pierce, moved by the now serious state of Grove's affairs, attempted to help. In the last two months of 1938, Ryerson accepted *Two Generations* for trade publication, undertook to reissue *A Search for America* using the sheets of the hapless Carrier edition, and on December 6, "confirming our understanding of your visits of last week and yesterday," proposed a plan for "the publication of your complete works now in print when you have completed their release from the present publishers." In the following months, Pierce acted as literary agent for Grove, not only selling the *Leonard Broadus* story for $120, but also arranging for the publishing of a short story in the *Canadian Bookman* for $30, writing hither and yon unsuccessfully trying to place "Murder in the Quarry" that Grove had brought out of his files, reading *Master of the Mill,* bringing out *America* and *Two Generations* by the beginning of August 1939, and parrying Grove's complaints throughout. Pierce could not interest any United States publisher in *Two Generations,* and sales within Canada were dismal, but Grove began asking for advances on his royalties and offered Pierce both his autobiography and the "Ant Book." On March 29, 1940, a sad and weary Pierce wrote, "If I can work a miracle for you in these vicious days, I shall."

But miracles were not for publishers. No one was interested in Grove's autobiography. All that Pierce could do—and did— was to sponsor Grove for election to the Royal Society. He was not elected until the next year, in April, and immediately he wrote Pierce, "I'd like to accept but there is a $20.00 fee and travelling expenses." Pierce had proposed him; what was he going to do about it?

This gracelessness from Grove followed upon an exchange that he and Pierce had been having for a month. Grove asked for release from Ryerson; Pierce pointed out that "we went to a good deal of expense in bringing your books under our imprint"; Grove retorted that Ryerson was not publishing anything; and Pierce put the situation bluntly: "Collaboration with the U.S. seems to be out of the question. I am doubtful whether publication independently in Canada of the sort of novel you write could be achieved without very heavy loss." At the beginning of May, Grove listed the manuscripts that Ryerson had. In addition to two hundred pages of the unfinished "Seasons," Ryerson had

"Murder in the Quarry," the "Ant Book," *Master of the Mill,* and "Felix Powell's Career." What was Ryerson going to do about them? Pierce wrote, "I feel we have got to do something and do it now for you." But the company did not agree, and by the beginning of July, Ryerson had declined to publish any of the manuscripts. The project of a collected edition was heard of no more. After the publishing flurry of 1939, and having managed to estrange Pierce a second time, Grove did not publish a book for five years.

CHAPTER 15

The Citizen

D URING THE years when the dream of the landed man of letters was fading, a variety of people did what they could to help Grove. In Toronto, Dr. Alexander, now in the last years of his long life and failing, nevertheless sent subscription forms for *Two Generations* to friends in universities from British Columbia to Cornell; Pelham Edgar who, with a few others, was working to establish a fund for the Canadian Writers' Foundation, spent much of his effort in trying to get some one to be responsible specifically for Grove; younger members of the English Department arranged to have articles by Grove published in the *Toronto Quarterly;* they put *A Search for America* on the required list for honors students; and they arranged for him to give an afternoon of lectures in January 1938. But visits with Toronto friends—Fairley or Pratt and so on—became rarer, letters were few, and Grove sometimes went for a year or more with no communication with them.

Nearer at hand, in London, Richard Crouch and his wife put Grove up when he went to the city on business or for physical checkups; they took parcels of books with them when they drove over to Simcoe; they lent the Groves their cottage at Rondeau Point for summer holidays; and when Mrs. Grove and Leonard joined the Anglican church in the spring of 1943, Crouch was godfather for Leonard. In Simcoe, the Naturalists' Club still took Grove with them on trips, but as Munro Landon said, "He couldn't hear the birds any longer. He couldn't get around. His back. His ears. He was too old for us to really have the good time we should have had. It all helped to make him bitter." [1] But he still told them romantic stories about himself and about his shadow family: "he told me he had two sons by his first marriage. They were both teachers; one, I believe, in Cincinnati, Ohio, the other, Stanford University. . . . Mr. Grove had not heard anything from them for a number of years." [2]

No amount of friendliness, however, could make up for a vanishing income. On doctor's orders in 1939, Grove gave up all pretense at farming and rented his acres, except for the land that the house and barn stood on. He kept a few cows, but part of his herd had died of disease. The school, too, was dwindling, even though it still followed the ideal of agricultural and manual training for the children: "we were exposed to a great deal. Whether it's important to know how to churn butter—I can do that too! They had a pretty much self-contained unit: they had chickens, they milked their own cows, churned their own butter, collected their own eggs. This was our practical work. We all had our lunch out there, so I suppose this helped with the food." [3] Apart from the fact that, as the Depression went on and the war began, fewer and fewer parents could afford the extra expense of a private school, facilities in the town schools were very much better than at the Groves' which was simply a one-room school with all its inadequacies transferred from West to East—another Falmouth or Haskett. Then too, discipline was severe, and Grove's temper was formidable: "He had no respect for a child's opinion. We were all in awe of him, in fact sometimes frightened. And we were this way because he could get angry if you didn't agree with him on something." [4] As the Simcoe children left, new recruits had to be found. The school changed its name to the F. P. Grove School and changed its direction to follow that of Froebel's Keilhau school, which took in as boarders children who were backward or who had learning problems of various kinds. Mrs. Grove proved to be particularly gifted in this work, and it provided her with income for many years.

For Grove, another possibility of making a livelihood, or even of beginning an entirely new career, appeared briefly with the provincial election of 1943. It was less than two weeks before the election on August 4 that Woodsworth's party, the CCF, decided to place a candidate in Grove's constituency, and when they asked him to run, he agreed. As with Abe Spalding, the district called, and he became a citizen. On the nomination papers he declared himself to be a farmer, and in the advertisement for the one address that there was time for him to give, he was announced as "Frederick Philip Grove, B.A., F.R.S.C." The Conservative won the seat as usual, with Grove 5,500 votes behind him, but he did get 2,107 votes, which, considering his brief candidacy and briefer campaign, was almost gratifying. In the following months he was appointed honorary president of the local CCF, he addressed luncheon meetings on their behalf, and he shared the platform on one occasion with Agnes McPhail. But none of the political activity brought in any money, and it was obviously not leading to a career.

As for royalties, by Lorne Pierce's account, the sales of Grove's books for 1943 were *Fruits of the Earth,* 41 copies; *A Search for America,* 73 copies; and *Two Generations,* 68 copies. Grove was in his mid-sixties. At the beginning of 1944, he again tried the scheme of a limited author's edition paid for by private subscription, to lessen costs for a publisher. Again, it worked. This time he approached Miss Ellen Elliot of Macmillan, who had been appointed a director of the company after Hugh Eayrs's death in 1940. The book was *The Master of the Mill.* Macmillan accepted it on Miss Elliot's recommendation and brought out the trade edition at the end of that year. After five years, Grove had published another book.

Early in 1944 another piece of good fortune came that made a great difference to the remaining years of Grove's life. Pelham Edgar finally established a fund for the Canadian Writers' Foundation, Inc., and in March Grove was made one of the three beneficiaries. He was sent a check for $200, the first of the checks of a grant of $100 a month which the foundation paid until the end of 1948, the year in which he died.

In the next month there came what Grove called "the appalling surprise," a crippling stroke which he suffered on April 14. In the face of that disaster, Grove showed himself at his best. Less than a week later, Mrs. Grove wrote to their old friend, Watson Kirkconnell, "His right side is paralysed though his mind has remained perfectly clear. In fact, he has read and reported (by dictation, his speech came back rapidly) one manuscript since." By June, although he was typing "with one finger of my left hand," as he told Crouch, he was walking with the help of a cane, and by the end of 1945, "my daily walk reached one mile."

Indeed, by the end of 1945, prospects were beginning to look almost hopeful again. In Ellen Elliot, Grove had found another devoted publisher. She not only reinstated him as a reader for Macmillan, but, like Lorne Pierce, she searched out other ways to help him earn a little money. Her most courageous action, however, was to give Grove contracts for both the "Ant Book" and his autobiography by mid-December 1945. But when, after all of her concern and efforts for him, she read the last eighty pages of the autobiography, she, like others before her, felt a little wistful: "As I read I was hoping perhaps to come across one little phrase mentioning the close friendship that undoubtedly does exist between Mr. Grove and ourselves now." [5] In the meantime, she had obtained for him a $500 advance on the two books she had just accepted; Macmillan paid him $109 royalties on *The Master* for the year; and the Writers' Foundation checks were coming along each month, so that Christmas of 1945 was one of the most cheerful that the Groves had had for some time.

The following May, Grove had another seizure. He could not walk, and his speech was henceforth unintelligible. Leonard, now sixteen, who had been sent to St. Andrews school for a year, returned home, and for over two years he tended his father—undressed him, bathed him, shaved him, put him to bed.[6] The end came on August 19, 1948. The body was taken to Rapid City and buried beside May's grave.

There had been honors to lighten the years: the medal from the Royal Society in 1934, an honorary life membership in the Canadian Authors' Association in 1939, membership in the Royal Society in 1941, the monthly grant from the Writers' Foundation beginning in 1944, an honorary degree from the University of Manitoba in 1946, and the governor-general's medal for nonfiction, awarded in 1947 for *In Search of Myself*. Few Canadians received such honors; possibly no one else in Grove's day received as many.

A few months before his final seizure, Grove asked Ellen Elliot to send back the manuscript of *Consider Her Ways* because he wanted to make some changes in the twenty-odd pages of the introduction. The introduction was the only part of the 1925 version of the "Ant Book" that had survived the revisions of the intervening years, and so these changes are of some importance, the more so since they are Grove's last comment. They are subtle and they are significant.

The ending is changed. In the other version, the aged ant-

scholar died, having completed her task of passing on her knowledge, and the introduction closed with "Peace be to her dust."
Now the pathetic disappears; there is no death scene, only the ambiguous ongoing of life. That change in tone and in meaning takes less than half a dozen lines.

It takes as many pages to achieve the other main change. It has to do with the means by which man and ant communicate. In the early version there is an elaborate scheme, a sort of parlor game, taking up seven or eight pages altogether, in which the trivial machinery is as painstaking as it is tiresome, and its effect is to underline the impossibility, the unreality of such a happening. In the final introduction all of the ingenious devices are cut, and in their stead is a conception that was a profound reality to Grove from the time of our first knowledge of him. It is that of the unity of nature, which goes back at least as far as the incident of the snakes in Haskett. The astonishing thing is how simply this is done, and once done, how logical it seems to be. There is no need for devices. All nature is one. There is a communion too deep for words.

The effect of this change is to create again a figure of multiple oneness, this time a fusion of authors. There is the I-narrator who is the ant-scholar, and there is the I-narrator who is the amateur myrmecologist who traveled to Venezuela, the obedient human scribe to whom this adventure happened. This narrator signs the introduction *F. P. G.*, but F. P. G. is both fictional and real, an embodiment of the life of the man who called himself Grove. He is man-traveler and ant-traveler, fictional narrator and Frederick Philip Grove, the name that appears on the title page.

The fusion and the resulting ambiguity are latent in the carefully plotted revolution of values which takes up the greater part of the introduction and is common to both versions. The amateur naturalist watching ants in the valley of the Orinoco is the outsider, the spectator sitting tailor-fashion (the Buddha pose), a gigantic isosceles triangle towering above the animalcules: man, the apex of creation. He says matter of factly that "even uneventful hours served to establish a certain relationship between the ant and myself" and that he developed "a power of subconsciously keeping an eye on the ants." The shift between ant and man begins very quietly when he first notices "a number of huge ants" with "enormous triangular heads, apex down and base up."

The adjectives in the factual observation show the changing ratio in physical size, coinciding with the changing values implied in the reversed triangle. The sense of human diminution is intensified by the giant trees of the surrounding tropical forest, and the small intruder finds himself in "the grip of primitive disquietudes . . . being surveyed and appraised by alien eyes." His self-confidence is further shaken when one of the ants, waving her antennae and fixing him with her shining eyes whose "glint and glitter seemed so human," mesmerizes him so that he realizes "Something uncanny had unbalanced me. . . . I felt as though I were in the power of these ants." The transformation continues that night in his dreams: "all night long, I dreamed of gigantic ants, ants the size of elephants . . . holding me at bay with their huge, trunklike, waving antennae." The physical exchange is complete; the man no longer dominates in size or strength.

But man's great claim to be the crown of creation lies in his unconquerable mind, and "my mind, however, was singularly free and mobile; and this gave me a queer sensation: much as a paralytic may contrast his mental agility with his muscular rigidity." The ants return to their campaign. This time, three ants crawl out on a limb and range themselves in front of his face: "They formed a short isosceles triangle with its apex down," a trinity of inverted triangles, within a fourth. The progress of their victory is detailed: "I must have fallen into a state next to actual sleep or anaesthesia. My eyes were open. Moments of clear but vacant consciousness were obliterated by lapses of an absolute mental void." Attempting to rise, the man falls and strikes his head. "On awaking I had had a very peculiar sensation. I had not seemed to be I" (xxviii). The ants have conquered his mind.

Up to this point, Grove had cut about two pages from the earlier script, which focused attention on the parlor game and so lost the force of the quite remarkable "I had not seemed to be I." With these words, the metamorphosis is almost complete, but it is not a descent such as Kafka's Gregor Samsa experienced; rather, it is an elevation, part of the ironic intent, from man to ant.

Following up the implications of the statement, Grove reshaped the ending, cutting out another five pages of contrivances, his changes having the curious effect of casting light behind them so that the earlier part, here recounted, gains in significance. The new ending, of less than four pages, details the movement from general metamorphosis to complete fusion, and it dwells upon the whole question of identity: "By some mesmeric action I, my individuality, had been sucked up or down into an alien mass-consciousness which communed with me through channels other than those of the senses. The moment I surrendered myself, my consciousness was that, not of my former self, but that of ants, and of no individual ant, so far, but of all antdom." The unity of nature has triumphed and F. P. G. goes on to the "mesmeric transposition of personality" with the ant-scholar of "extreme old age." It was perhaps a compliment to F. P. G. that the mind he fused with was that of a dean of scholars.

At the same time, the fall in which he struck his head keeps the action within the ambiguous real-fictional world of the real-fictional writer, and so there is an easy reasonableness in the age-old dream-vision as the vehicle for ant wisdom. F. P. G. absorbed Wawa-quee's six-year expedition during a trance that "seemed to extend over years and years; in reality it was probably comprised within minutes or even seconds," for time too has become ambivalent. When he returned to his Venezuelan host, "I knew that I was not yet I. I walked and acted like a human being; but my mind was that of the ant: I had lived her life; and her memory was mine." The figurative statement once more implies factual reality, and the identification strengthens the personal analogies within the story.

The question of the individual and his identity that this fusion of all nature and all F. P. G.'s throws into relief had occupied Grove even from the 1913 letters when he said, "I could never be a citizen," for he would not sacrifice his individuality, the I-myself. It is a theme that he repeatedly probed from Phil Branden and his waiter friend on; it was in Grove's pseudonymous life. In these final changes, however, Branden's "I must be I" has a shifting echo in "I had not seemed to be I," "I knew that I was not yet I." Indeed, Grove seems to be amused at the I-not-I frenzy. If "life in all its forms is one," if one form of it flows into another and can take the shape of another, the mind of another, what price the individual, or the pose he assumes, or his name? "I surrendered myself."

CHAPTER 16

Conclusion

GROVE WAS as much a realist as Wordsworth was. He was no more a regionalist than Hemingway was. He carried his world of ideas with him and placed them against many physical settings, fictional or otherwise, from South America to Amaranth, from Banff to Hamburg. He experimented with many ways of expressing them—in animal fable, in exotic symbolism, in domestic tales, in sentimental journeys, in analyses of snowdrifts. He picked up hints hither and yon, from Hardy, from Hamsun, from Wells, from Mann, and he had a love affair with Cabell. But the origin of his world of ideas lay in the writings of Rousseau and Thoreau, Froebel and Herbart, Darwin, Bates and Belt, and the philosophical myrmecologist Wheeler. These writings are the significant context of his thought, and they provided his training and his abiding interests.

Rousseau's two Discourses and his *Emile*, together with Thoreau's *Walden*, provided most of the ideas to be found in Grove's novels, while nineteenth-century theories of elementary education gave particular direction to this "Professor of Science" in the emphasis on mathematics and nature study, and in the doctrine of cultural epochs being mirrored in the individual life. Enveloping all of these ideas was the concept of evolution, which Grove made most explicit in *The Master of the Mill*.

It is largely because of Grove's preoccupation with the great visions of nineteenth-century science that his novels concentrate on the themes of changing generations and shifting cultural epochs, which in turn dictate the chronicle form of the passing years. Similarly, it is his concern with the human race rather than with people that in part accounts for the abstract "schematic figures" that exemplify his theses. Finally, this preoccupation explains Grove's constant longing to embrace vastness, the huge designs that he drew up for his work, from the first trilogy,

"Latter-Day Pioneers," to the final, unfinished, all-inclusive "The Seasons."

The designs are often fascinating, but here the archetypal approach is deceptive, for frequently the completed work is, as Grove said of one of them, "good in the skeleton, doubtful in the flesh." [1] Part of the discrepancy between the dream and its realization lay in Grove's reluctance to admit his limitations, and closely allied to that, in his pretensions to experience or knowledge that he quite clearly did not have. But there is also a curious correspondence between the vision and its tawdry clothing in his writing and the dualism within Grove himself: "The whole man and writer was a complex being: he combined the high qualities of seer and savant with the suspicions and envies and intolerances of a frustrated villager." [2] The dualism is reflected everywhere in his work, in the two-part structure of most of the novels, in opposing modes of life, in fixed contrasts of characters, in the whole night-and-day, good-and-evil, Mary-Eve, either-or world that he creates. It is a world at variance with his beginning and ending theme of the unity of nature. But then even within such unity, there is no ideal world. The ant world is a wise, communal, desirable society, but it harbors ambition, treachery, and murder. Probably the most remarkable example of Grove's dualism is the man himself who constantly asserted his unyielding individuality while he went to extraordinary lengths to hide his identity.

It may be that it is when he has only one layer of actor to deal with, when he is writing through an I-narrator, that he is most at ease. At any rate, it is notable that *Over Prairie Trails,* at least in its beginning, and *A Search for America* and *Consider Her Ways* have a poise that is not often found in the other books. Moreover, the lively, vigorous, varied narrative of the last two shows Grove's craftsmanship at its best. Elsewhere, there are scenes that are moving or haunting or powerful even in the midst of the tawdry.

Grove's awareness of his failures is expressed most poignantly in a passage in the 1925 version of the "Ant Book," when he speaks of "the darkest of all those features which make human life the inexorable, bitter, and contemptible thing which it is. . . . In the last resort, he who wins the great prizes of life, namely real achievement and real greatness, will do so by no virtue of his own, for even the industrious owe their industry to things beyond their control. . . . One will with or without effort, turn the thoughts into immortal treasures of deed or words; the other will strive and struggle and yet, by some freak of heredity, always fall short of the highest achievement; the one will reap where the other merely sowed. Such is Nature's relentless law" (170–71).

Notes and References

Preface

1. "The Grove Enigma Resolved," by Douglas O. Spettigue; *Queen's Quarterly*, Vol. 79, No. 1 (April 1972), pp. 1–2. Pre-1913 details in the Chronology are also taken from this source.

Chapter One

1. Twice in the attendance record for the six months, January to June 1913, the signature *Fred P. Grove* appears.

2. "The Mennonites of Manitoba," by Prof. H. L. Sawatsky, *Echo Centennial Supplement*, Altona (November 25, 1970), p. 7.

3. *Inspectors' Reports of Bi-Lingual School Districts, 1915*, Public Archives of Manitoba.

4. Remarks are taken from tapes made during July 1970. Tape 2/B: Mrs. Toews and Mrs. Hiebert of Steinbach, originally of Haskett and also former students of Grove at Winkler. Mrs. Hiebert is a retired schoolteacher. Tape 5/A: John Warkentin of Winnipeg, retired assistant professor of Education, University of Manitoba. His father was a member of Grove's Haskett school board and uncle to I. J. Warkentin.

5. Tape 4/B Jacob Giesbrecht, Winnipeg, July 1970.

6. Correspondence: I. J. Warkentin to M. S., April 25, 1971.

7. When I visited the late Mr. I. J. Warkentin in July 1970, he showed me these letters and lent them to me. In the spring of 1971 he generously donated them to the Grove Collection. They are dated September 7, October 20, November 1, December 6 in 1913, and February 10, 1914.

8. Tape 5/A Abram Kroeker, Winnipeg, July 1970.

9. Correspondence as in n. 6.

10. "Frederick Philip Grove" by B. Warkentin, B.A., *The Manitoba School Journal*, Vol. 9, No. 5 (April 1947), p. 8.

Chapter Two

1. "The Entrance Examinations," by Fred Grove, *The Western School Journal*, Vol. IX (November 1914), pp. 241–44.

2. *The Educational Ideas of Pestalozzi and Froebel*, by F. H. Hayward. London: Ralph, Holland, 1905, p. 13.

3. "Jean Jacques Rousseau als Erziehert" von Fred Grove, Hauptlehrer an der Mittelschule zu Winkler, Man., *Der Nordwesten*, November 15, December 2, 9, 16. The translations are mine.

4. *Rousseau's Emile or Treatise on Education*, Abridged, translated, and annotated by William H. Payne, Ph.D., LL.D., chancellor of the University of Nashville and president of the Peabody Normal College; International Education Series edited by William T. Harris. New York: Appleton, 1893.

Chapter Three

1. "Education in Virden" by the Reverend R. O. Armstrong, *The Empire Advance*, August 24, 1915, p. 1.

2. "Grove, Fred P. (Ex-M.) Virden," Students in Attendance: Arts, 1915–16; *University of Manitoba Annual Calendar, Session 1916–17*, p. 159. Since Grove had established Professional Class 2 standing (Grade 11) by passing half of Grade 12 and a normal school course, there was no problem about his admission. In any case, by this stage in the war, students who had come from Europe and whose records were impossible to get were being admitted on a trial basis. If they made good, no further questions were asked about previous schooling.

3. Teacher accreditation card for Catherine Grove (née Tena Wiens), Department of Youth and Education, government of Manitoba.

4. Correspondence: Mrs. Fred Irwin to M. S., August 19, 1970, and W. M. Scarth to M. S., October 18, 1970.

5. Remarks from teachers and students at Virden are taken from tapes made during the summer of 1970. The teachers are: W. P. Johnson of Winnipeg, who substituted during Grove's illness, Tape 12/B, September 26/70; Miss E. Gilray, the language teacher, now in Toronto, Tape 8/B, July 31/70; and Mrs. Myrtle McNiven of Brandon, who was the public school principal at the time, Tape 11/B, September 23/70.

6. Tape 3/A, Bruce Mackenzie, Gladstone, July 8, 1970.

7. "Grove, Frederick P. (Ex-M.) Gladstone," Students in Attendance: Arts, 1916–17; *University of Manitoba Annual Calendar, Session 1917–18*, p. 162. Also, *Report of the University Faculty to the*

Notes and References

Council for the Session of 1916–17, p. 44, Report of the Department of German, "One extra-mural student is included in the attendance for the Third Year."

8. *University of Manitoba Convocation Program and Class and Honour lists 1916–17*. Scholarships. Arts. Third Year. Full details of standing in each course, with the names of the students, are given for French, p. 34; for German, p. 35. In the previous year, the gold medalist in German was Paul Hiebert, author of *Sarah Binks*.

9. "Gladstone School Report for September," *Gladstone Age*, October 11, 1917.

10. The quotations that follow are taken from taped conversations held during the summer of 1970 in the Falmouth-Amaranth area and elsewhere in Manitoba where former Falmouth-Ferguson pupils could be found. The tapes are 5/B, 6/A and B, 8/A.

11. Tape 4/A, Mrs. Gunn, Winnipeg, July 12, 1970.

12. Letters from McClelland & Stewart to Grove, in the Grove Collection. Unfortunately, the publisher some years ago destroyed their early files, so that Grove's letters to them do not exist.

13. This letter from John Burroughs is also in the Grove Collection.

14. "Schedule of Salaries," *The Western School Journal*, Vol. XIV, No. 6, p. 329.

15. Correspondence: Victor Suddaby to M.S., August 8, 1970.

Part Two

1. The estimates of the chronology of the works are based on the references that Grove makes in letters to A. L. Phelps and on references which publishers make to MSS Grove sent them or wrote them about.

2. Script of the CBS Symposium, September 1962, "In Search of Frederick Philip Grove," p. 14.

Chapter Four

1. All page references are to the New Canadian Library edition of *A Search for America*, Toronto: McClelland & Stewart, 1971.

2. *Amerika* by Franz Kafka, New York: New Directions, 1946. Preface by Klaus Mann, p. xii, p. i.

Chapter Five

1. Of these four books, two are available in New Canadian Library reprints: *Over Prairie Trails*, 1957; and *Settlers of the Marsh*, 1966. The other two have not been reprinted: *The Turn of the Year*, Mc-

Clelland & Stewart, 1923; and *The Yoke of Life*, Macmillan, 1930. My page references are to these editions.

2. Correspondence: A. L. Phelps to Grove, August 12, 1925, saying that he had read the manuscript.

3. Henry David Thoreau, *Walden*. London: Dent, 1908, p. 119.

4. *The Temptation of St. Anthony: The Complete Works of Gustave Flaubert* (trans.), ed. Ferdinand Brunetière. New York and London: M. Walter Dunne, 1904, Vol. VII, pp. 42–43; 38.

5. J. J. Rousseau, *The Social Contract and Discourse on the Origin of Inequality*, ed. Lester G. Crocker. New York: Washington Square Press, 1967, p. 227.

Chapter Six

1. Tape 12/A, Professor Ernest Birkinshaw, Brandon University, September 25, 1970.

2. Tape 12/A, Mrs. Elizabeth Barrett Eastgate, Brandon, September 24, 1970.

3. It is doubtful if Grove ever destroyed anything that he wrote. In the Grove Collection there are essays, addresses, and the occasional short story that he used over and over again, sometimes changing the opening sentence to suit a new set of circumstances, sometimes changing only the title.

4. Grove's short stories have only recently been published in book form: *Tales from the Margin: The Selected Short Stories of Frederick Philip Grove*, ed. Desmond Pacey. Toronto: Ryerson, 1971. The page references for "The Boat" are to this volume.

5. A review by Grove of *Captain Salvation*, by Frederick W. Wallace, *The Canadian Bookman*, September 1925, p. 148.

6. W. A. Deacon quoted this sentence from Cabell's *The High Place*, p. 134, in his review of the book in *Saturday Night*, June 21, 1924, p. 8. It may have been Deacon's enthusiasm for Cabell that led Grove to make this attempt.

7. Correspondence: Grove to Kirkconnell, January 11, 1927.

Chapter Seven

1. "Economics," *Walden*, p. 12.

Chapter Eight

1. Tape 3/B, Mrs. Mackenzie, Neepawa, July 20, 1970.
2. Tape 12/A, Professor Ernest Birkinshaw.
3. Tape 6/B, Ernest Birkinshaw, Sr., Rapid City, July 23, 1970.

4. The death certificate gives as cause of death, "Acute appendicitis with perforation and general peritonitis," and contributing cause, "Acute oedema of lungs." The racial origin of Phyllis May is given as Dutch.

Chapter Nine

1. Tape 11/A, Graham Spry, Ottawa, August 20, 1970.
2. Correspondence: H. C. Miller to Grove, February 12, 1928.

Chapter Ten

1. Rousseau, *The Social Contract*, p. 212.
2. Page references to *Fruits of the Earth* are to the New Canadian Library edition. Toronto: McClelland & Stewart, 1965.

Chapter Eleven

1. Correspondence: W. A. Deacon to Lorne Pierce, September 10, 1959.
2. "The Graphic Publishers Limited, Ottawa, Ontario, Canada, 1924–32," by Erik Spicer. Unpublished research paper for the Department of Library Science, University of Michigan, August 1951, 47 pp.; p. 9.
3. Correspondence: Department of Consumer and Corporate Affairs, to M.S., August 27, 1970.

Chapter Twelve

1. Tape 11/A, Graham Spry, Ottawa, August 20, 1970.
2. "F. P. Grove and the Graphic Press," by Wilfrid Eggleston, *The Ottawa Journal*, March 4, 1967.
3. Tape 10/B, Wilfrid Eggleston, Ottawa, August 20, 1970.
4. *Stephen Leacock, A Check-list and Index of His Writings* by Dr. Gerhard R. Lomer, 1954; quoted by Dora Rideout Hood, *The Side Door*. Toronto: Ryerson, 1958, p. 78; and by Erik Spicer, p. 15.
5. Erik Spicer, p. 38.
6. Correspondence: Raymond Knister to W. Kennedy, November 28, 1931. National Archives of Canada, Canadian Authors' Association file, MG. 28, Case E 2, Vol. 1: Failure of Graphic Publishers Limited in 1932.
7. Ibid., Trustee's Statement of Affairs.
8. A. L. Phelps, *Canadian Writers*. Toronto: McClelland & Stewart, 1951, p. 39.

Chapter Thirteen

1. Correspondence: F. P. Grove to Richard Crouch, March 28, 1936.
2. *The Simcoe Reformer*, February 18, 1932.
3. Tape 9/B, Munro Landon, Simcoe, August 15, 1970.
4. Tape 10/B, Leonard Grove, Toronto, August 17, 1970.

Chapter Fourteen

1. Tape 14/A, Professor W. Mackay, dean of law, University of Western Ontario, London, October 26, 1970.
2. Robert Ayre, "Frederick Philip Grove: Canadian Writers of Today," *The Canadian Forum* (April 1932), pp. 255–57. The verse, "From The Dirge," by Frederick Philip Grove, pp. 257–60.
3. *Consider Her Ways*. Toronto: Macmillan, 1947, pp. 169–70. The page references are to the published version which is very close to the 1933 manuscript version of the work.
4. Fr. Sumichrast, "Notes of the Habits of Certain Species of MEXICAN HYMENOPTERA," *Transactions Of The American Entomological Society*, Vol. 2 (1868), pp. 39–46. Sumichrast's article is included in Wheeler's bibliography.
5. Correspondence: Macmillan Company to Grove, March 28, 1944.
6. Spettigue's announcement, made after the text of this book was written, that Grove's given names were *Felix Paul* points up how very close Grove came to revealing his identity in the title of this story.
7. Page references are to *In Search of Myself*. Toronto: Macmillan, 1946.

Chapter Fifteen

1. Tape 9/B, Munro Landon.
2. Script of the CBC Symposium, "In Search of Frederick Philip Grove," p. 12.
3. Tape 14/A, Professor Mackay.
4. Tape 14/B, Mrs. J. Raymer, Toronto, October 27, 1970.
5. Correspondence: Ellen Elliot to Carleton Stanley, February 1, 1946.

Chapter Sixteen

1. "Frederick Philip Grove: A Group of Letters" by Desmond Pacey, *Canadian Literature*, No. 11 (Winter, 1962), pp. 28–38, p. 36.
2. "Philip Grove," by Wilfrid Eggleston, *Winnipeg Free Press*, September 6, 1948.

Selected Bibliography

PRIMARY SOURCES

1. *Published Books*

Consider Her Ways. Toronto: Macmillan, 1947.

Fruits of the Earth. Toronto and London: Dent, 1933. New Canadian Library edition, with Introduction by G. M. Park, Toronto: McClelland & Stewart, 1965.

In Search of Myself. Toronto: Macmillan, 1946.

It Needs to Be Said. Toronto and New York: Macmillan, 1929.

The Master of the Mill. Author's limited edition, 1944. Trade edition, Toronto: Macmillan, 1944. New Canadian Library edition, with Introduction by R. E. Waters, Toronto: McClelland & Stewart, 1961.

Our Daily Bread. Toronto: Macmillan, 1928. London: Jonathan Cape, 1928.

Over Prairie Trails. Toronto: McClelland & Stewart, 1922. Reissued, Toronto: Macmillan, 1929. New Canadian Library edition, with Introduction by Malcolm Ross, Toronto: McClelland & Stewart, 1957.

A Search for America. Ottawa: The Graphic Publishers, 1927. American edition, New York and Montreal: Louis Carrier, 1928. Carrier edition reissued, Toronto: Ryerson, 1939. School edition, abridged by J. F. Swayze, Toronto: Ryerson, 1947. New Canadian Library edition, with Introduction by Stanley E. McMullin, Toronto: McClelland & Stewart, 1971.

Settlers of the Marsh. Toronto: Ryerson; New York: Doran, 1925. New Canadian Library edition, with Introduction by Thomas Saunders, Toronto: McClelland & Stewart, 1966.

Tales from the Margin: The Selected Short Stories of Frederick Philip Grove, edited by Desmond Pacey. Toronto: Ryerson, 1971.

The Turn of the Year. Toronto: McClelland & Stewart, 1923. Reissued by Macmillan, 1929.

Two Generations. Author's limited edition, 1939. Trade edition, Toronto: Ryerson, 1939.

The Yoke of Life. Toronto: Macmillan; New York: Richard Smith, 1930.

2. *Main Unpublished Works* (in rough chronological order)

"MAN, His Habits, Social Organisation, and Outlook," c. 1925. The first version of the "Ant Book," later called *Consider Her Ways.*

"The Canyon: A Romance and Its Sequel." Grove's attempt at James Branch Cabell's manner. Submitted to Ryerson.

"Murder in the Quarry." An attempt at a popular detective novel. Submitted to Ryerson.

"The Weatherhead Fortunes," c. 1927–28. Following upon *Our Daily Bread,* the town part of the country-town-city western trilogy. Submitted to both Ryerson and Graphic Publishers.

"Jane Atkinson." The city part of the threesome.

"Felix Powell's Career." Submitted to Ryerson for publication, but rejected. Said to have been destroyed later by Mrs. Grove.

"The Seasons." Unfinished. Panoramic, cross-section view of the life of Ontario.

SECONDARY SOURCES

1. *Books*

PACEY, DESMOND. *Frederick Philip Grove.* Toronto: Ryerson, 1945. Takes pride of place as the first book about Grove. Written during Grove's lifetime and with his cooperation. Strongly under the spell of Grove's view of himself and his works.

SPETTIGUE, DOUGLAS O. *Frederick Philip Grove.* Toronto: Copp Clark, 1969. After nearly a quarter of a century, a second book on Grove. Perceptive criticism of the writing but mainly concerned with demonstrating that Grove's account of his early life cannot be substantiated. Important in helping to clear the way for fresh examinations of the nature of Grove's thinking.

SUTHERLAND, RONALD. *Frederick Philip Grove.* Toronto: McClelland & Stewart, 1969. 62 pp. A monograph in the Canadian Writers series. Sees Grove's novels as theses and his characters as symbols. Suggests an affinity between Grove and French Canadian novelists of the soil.

2. *Additional Articles*

Frederick Philip Grove. Edited by Desmond Pacey in the series, Critical Views on Canadian Writers. Toronto: Ryerson, 1970. A useful book, about equally divided between reviews of Grove's books as they appeared and representative articles, though only three are after 1950. "A Solitary Giant," by Robert Ayre, that so incensed Grove, is included; so are excerpts from Phelps and Eggleston; and "A Novelist as Poet," by Thomas Saunders says what can be said for Grove's verse.

HOLLIDAY, W. B. "Frederick Philip Grove, An Impression." *Canadian Literature*, No. 3 (Winter 1960), 17–22. An intimate glimpse of Grove by a young writer who went to work for him briefly in the fall of 1939 and later corresponded with him.

MCMULLIN, STANLEY E. "Grove and the Promised Land." *Canadian Literature*, No. 49 (Summer 1971), 10–19. An extension of the Introduction to *A Search for America*. The loss of the ideal world.

NESBITT, BRUCE. " 'The Seasons,' Grove's Unfinished Novel." *Canadian Literature*, No. 18 (Autumn 1963), 47–51. An account of events and characters in the existing manuscript.

PACEY, DESMOND. "Frederick Philip Grove, A Group of Letters," *Canadian Literature*, No. 11 (Winter 1962), 28–38. The letters from Grove before and during Pacey's writing of the 1945 book on Grove. A number of Grove's comments on his novels.

SAUNDERS, DORIS. "The Grove Collection of Papers in the University of Manitoba: A Tentative Evaluation." *Bibliographical Society of Canada Papers* (1963), pp. 7–20. Some details have been changed after further investigation of the papers, but this remains the only extensive account of the purchase of the Grove Papers and the contents of the collection at that time.

SIROIS, ANTOINE. "Grove et Ringuet: Témoins d'une époque." *Canadian Literature*, No. 49 (Summer 1971), 20–27. A comparison between Ringuet's *Trente Arpents* and Grove's *Fruits of the Earth*, viewing both novels as novels of the soil treating the time of transition from the agricultural to the technical age.

SPETTIGUE, DOUGLAS O. " 'Frederick Philip Grove,' " *Queen's Quarterly*, Vol. 78, No. 4 (December 1971), pp. 614–15. Spettigue's first indication that he had discovered Grove's identity.

——— "The Grove Enigma Resolved," *Queen's Quarterly*, Vol. 79, No. 1 (April 1972), pp. 1–2. The announcement of Grove's date of birth, name, parentage, and early activities.

See also introductory essays to individual works in the Canadian Library editions.

Index

Index

17, 76, 84, 97-98, 188, mansion symbol, 77, 82, 103, 130, 157, 169, 174; teacher of nature study and mathematics, 27-28, 30, 31, 34, 37, 42, 45, 49, 71, 75, 90, 91, 160, 188, *see also* educational philosophy, Nature, Mathematics; teaching certification, 29, 54; transmigration, 29, 185; university career, 42-43, 46, 54, 184; Virden, 42-45, 51; Winkler, 17, 29-35, 42, 44, 91, 115

THEMES:
adolescence, 40-41, 69, 83, 84, 86, 105; agricultural ideal, 60, 61, 66, 76, 81, 88, 100, 103, 109, 157-58, 169; biological re-organization of human race, 109, 163-64; dualism (contrasts), 61, 80, 96, 97, 103, 110, 130-31, 175, 189; evolution, 37, 69, 172-73, 188; generation conflict, 27, 101, 130, 168, 175, 188, *see also* generations trilogy; hermaphroditic figure, 81, 88, 97, 104, 170, 172, 173, *see also* primordial creator; individual, the child, 103, 105, 169, "I, myself", 39, 66, 103, 105, 108-9, 169, 187, "I not I", 73, 77, 88, 186, 187, metamorphosis (self-realization, transformation), 37, 57, 59, 60, 66-69, 84, 86, 101, 129, 186-87, nature of, 68-69, 73, 79, 88, 110, 169, 175, and nature, 70, 71, 72, 85, 97, versus citizen, 39, 57, 58, 61, 107, 129, 130, 187; love, brother-sister, 97, 168, 170, male-female, 40, 76, 80-82, 84, 95, 96-97, 103, 106, 108, 109-10, 130-31, 169, 175, son-mother, 97, 106-7; pioneering, 168; primordial creator, 88, 170, 172, 173, *see also* hermaphroditic figure; sex, *see* love, dualism; slavery, 81-82, 88, 100, 101, 129, 175; trilogy, generations (*Our Daily Bread*, "The Weatherhead Fortunes", "Jane Atkinson"), 39, 57, 58, 101-10, 129,

130, 168, Marshland (*Over Prairie Trails, The Turn Of The Year, Settlers Of The Marsh, The Yoke Of Life*), 57, 58, 70-88; world-within-world, 71, 82, 103; *see also* Nature, Cultural Epochs, German Educational Philosophy, Grove's educational philosophy, symbolism

WORKS:
The Adventure of Leonard Broadus, 176, 179
"Ant Book", *see Consider Her Ways* (1933), "MAN, His Habits, Social Organization, and Outlook" (1925)
"The Canyon, or The Poet's Dream: A Romance And Its Sequel", 95-98, 101, 106, 107, 108, 110, 131, 140, 164
Consider Her Ways (1933 "Ant Book", *see also* "MAN, His Habits, Social Organization, and Outlook"), 64, 99, 162-67, 179, 180, 184, 184-87, 189
"The Entrance Examinations", 36-37, 160
"Felix Powell's Career", 176, 180
Fruits Of The Earth ("The Chronicle of Spalding District", "Abe Spalding, Pioneer"), 27, 57, 58, 93, 124, 128-31, 144, 146, 162, 168, 182, 183
"How To Appreciate Literature", 159
It Needs To Be Said ("Addresses Not Delivered"), 58, 92, 121, 126-28, 143, 159; "The Novel", 92; *see also* "Nationhood", "How To Appreciate Literature"
"Jane Atkinson", 57, 102, 107-10, 128, 129, 164, 175
"MAN His Habits, Social Organization, and Outlook" (1925 "Ant Book", *see also Consider Her Ways*), 58, 71, 98-100, 162, 165, 176, 184-87, 189-90

Index